*The minister is called upon to form and inform the people. Again and again we are reassured by Robert Schuller that he has heard the call and taken the leap of faith to answer it. His own spiritual autobiography leads us, the readers, without ceasing into prayerful positions in our thoughts and in our actions.*
—Dr. Maya Angelou
Writer/Professor

*In both his ministry and this compelling odyssey, Dr. Schuller powerfully teaches what he has learned "the old-fashioned way": Until we feel the pulse of God, we really don't feel the pulse of His children. The Brotherhood of Man flows out of the prayer-gained sense of the Fatherhood of God.*
—Dr. Stephen R. Covey
Author of *The 7 Habits of Highly Effective People*

*Robert Schuller has pulled back the drapes and allowed us to peek into the window of his life. What we see could not be more inspiring and challenging: a leader molded from the crucible of prayer!*
—C. Peter Wagner
Professor of Church Growth,
Fuller Theological Seminary

*Dr. Schuller's book* Prayer: My Soul's Adventure with God *could well be entitled* Walking and Talking with God—From the Valleys to the Mountaintops. *It portrays an intimate relationship and a man's life story, with full exposure of his faith, his family, and his future. Fascinating, informative, and encouraging reading that shows us the way to deeper faith and a more meaningful walk with God.*
—Zig Ziglar
Author and Motivational
Teacher

*This is a beautiful book of value to all people. Regardless of your race, creed, or religion, you will find guidance through the adversity and afflictions we are all subject to. Robert Schuller's newest book reaches beyond religion and information to what we all need—spirituality, inspiration, and understanding. Read it and live a life with meaning.*
—Dr. Bernie Siegel
Surgeon, Author of *Love, Medicine, and Miracles*

*Bob Schuller has been a friend of mine for almost two decades. I know him to be an earnest man after God's own heart, committed to stimulating the minds and hearts of people all over the world through his own unique efforts in preaching and teaching. Through exposure to his family, I know him and his wife, Arvella, to be devoted to the endeavor of prayer. I am sure the readers of this book will be enriched.*

—John Wimber
International Director of the
Association of Vineyard
Churches

*How wonderful! In a powerfully practical explanation, offered with gentle humility, the prayer keys Bob Schuller has found release the kind of ceaseless creativity God has worked through his life!* —Jack W. Hayford, D. Litt
Senior Pastor, The Church
on the Way
Van Nuys, California

*The heart of a pastor with the zeal of an evangelist. Dr. Robert Schuller is one of the greatest Christian leaders of our time. His message of God's love transcends denominational barriers and brings hope to a hurting world in need of a Savior.* —Paul F. Crouch
Founder and President of
Trinity Broadcasting Network

*Anything the world-famous preacher/pastor Robert Schuller writes is fascinating and inspiring to the whole world. How much more so when the book concerns his soul's adventure with God. Anyone who reads this masterpiece will be infinitely encouraged in the Lord and in the life-changing power of prayer.* —W. A. Criswell
Pastor Emeritus, First Baptist
Church of Dallas

*An absolutely thrilling journey into the life of one of the greatest men of God in the twentieth century.* —Peter Lowe
President and CEO of Peter
Lowe International

*As a man's prayer life grows and develops, so his ministry, preaching, and influence grow and develop. My good friend Dr. Schuller shares personal insights on the levels of prayer that he found to be powerful strengths in his life! This book is a must for every pastor and leader!*

—David Yonggi Cho
Senior Pastor of the Yoido
Full Gospel Church
Seoul, Korea

# PRAYER:
# MY SOUL'S ADVENTURE WITH GOD

# ROBERT H. SCHULLER

*This certificate certifies that this is an official hand-autographed
edition of* Prayer: My Soul's Adventure With God
*by Robert H. Schuller*

# PRAYER: MY SOUL'S ADVENTURE WITH GOD

*A Spiritual Autobiography*

# Other Books

## by Dr. Robert H. Schuller

*Tough Times Never Last But Tough People Do!,* 1983.
*Tough Minded Faith for Tender Hearted People,* 1984.
*The Power of Being Debt Free* with Paul D. Dunn, 1985.
*The Be-Happy Attitudes,* 1985.
*Be Happy You Are Loved,* 1986.
*Success Is Never Ending, Failure Is Never Final,* 1988.
*Believe in the God Who Believes in You,* 1989.
*Life's Not Fair But God Is Good,* 1991.

# PRAYER: MY SOUL'S ADVENTURE WITH GOD

*A Spiritual Autobiography*

# ROBERT H. SCHULLER

Thomas Nelson, Inc.
Nashville • Atlanta • London • Vancouver

Published in Nashville, Tennessee, by Thomas Nelson, Inc., and distributed in Canada by Word Communications, Ltd., Richmond, British Columbia, and in the United Kingdom by Word (UK), Ltd., Milton Keynes, England.

Unless otherwise noted, Scripture quotations are from the NEW KING JAMES VERSION of the Bible. Copyright © 1979, 1980, 1982, Thomas Nelson, Inc.

Scripture quotations noted TLB are from THE LIVING BIBLE. Copyright © 1971. Tyndale House Publishers, Inc., Wheaton, IL 60189. Used by permission.

Scripture quotations noted NEB are from THE NEW ENGLISH BIBLE. Copyright © 1961, 1970 by the Delegates of the Oxford University Press and the Syndics of the Cambridge University Press. Reprinted by permission.

Scripture quotations noted NIV are taken from the HOLY BIBLE, NEW INTERNATIONAL VERSION®. Copyright © 1973, 1978, 1984 by International Bible Society. Used by permission of Zondervan Bible Publishing House. All rights reserved.

The "NIV" and "New International Version" trademarks are registered in the United States Patent and Trademark Office by International Bible Society. Use of either trademark requires the permission of International Bible Society.

Poem by James Leigh Hunt in Chapter 1 is from *The New Oxford Book of English Verse, 1250–1950.* Ed. by Henlen Gardner, © 1972.

### Library of Congress Cataloging-in-Publication Data

Schuller, Robert Harold.
    Prayer : my soul's adventure with God / Robert H. Schuller.
      p.  cm.
    ISBN 0-7852-7777-3; 0-7852-7560-6 DLX; 0-7852-7582-7 FL;
      0-7852-7597-5 QVC
    1. Schuller, Robert Harold.   2. Reformed Church in America—
Clergy—Biography.  3. Spiritual biography—United States.   4. Prayer—
Christianity.  I. Title.
BX9543.S36A3   1995
285.7′092—dc20                             95–16941
                                               CIP

Printed in the United States of America
2 3 4 5 6 7 — 01 00 99 98 97 96 95

# Dedication

In these five strong Christian households, with our seventeen grandchildren, God lives and leads, answering our prayers.

Raise the curtain on tomorrow! It promises to be filled with powerful stories of positive possibilities unfolding in these five faithful families—for prayer leads them on. To God be the glory.

# Contents

## The Seven Levels of Effective Prayer

# Acknowledgments

## TO

*my secretary,*
*Barbara Ann Evans*

*Who painstakingly took all the words and scribbled*
*sentences from my handwritten yellow tablet and*
*entered them into the word processor.*

## TO

*my editor,*
*Bruce Nygren*

*Who patiently and professionally probed and*
*prodded this preacher's story until it became a book.*

## TO

*my wife,*
*Arvella DeHaan Schuller*

*Without whom this story would never have unfolded,*
*and this book could not and would not have been written.*

## TO

*The thousands of families and friends and faithful followers*
*whose prayers have moved God to sculpt a life and shape*
*a story that is good news.*

# *My Soul's Adventure!*

The title of this book is a crisp, truthful, "right on" summary of my life: *Prayer: my soul's adventure with God!*

I believe from the depths of my being that every soul on this planet longs for a similar adventure—the greatest adventure of all: *connecting with God.*

I believe that you long for that adventure.

This book, using key events of my life, points the way for *you,* through prayer, to have a dramatic, life-changing, uplifting adventure of your own with the God who loves you so much.

## The Truth about My Life

Yes, my life has been—and is—an adventure with God.

I never thought I'd write an autobiography. This—my thirtieth book—may come close to that.

I've always been reticent: Could any person really write an autobiography and be truly honest? I don't know. There are pitfalls and land mines for author and reader alike: Exposure. Vulnerability. Ego forces. False modesty. Calculated exaggerations. Name dropping. Boredom. Self-serving sentences to manipulate the reader's emotions. Self-serving statements that allow no reader to criticize or interrupt.

But others have tried to write my story. Biographers, they're called. They have written in unforgivable print what they have wanted without my having an opportunity to correct, question, criticize, or applaud. So—I've decided it's my turn.

This book will not be perfect. Intentionally or unintentionally, I will be guilty of sins of omission and commission. But I'll try my best.

I have a confession to make: I am addicted to a lifetime habit of being a pastor. I *really* want to help people who are hurting.

"Preach to broken hearts, and you'll always be up-to-date." Years ago I read these lines by Phillips Brooks, the great Episcopalian clergyman, as he addressed young students of the ministry.

Now I dedicate these pages to that pastoral purpose! May you find hope in your hurting or help in your dreaming from this true story of one man's prayer life.

So, back to this book's title, which tells the truth about my life. Each word is crucial:

**Prayer:**          **My earliest memory is of a childhood prayer, a request I made to God as a young boy. (I'll tell you about that prayer in the next chapter.) This simple request became my lifelong dream and passion. This prayer also contained the elementary structure that frames my "Possibility-Thinking" pattern of living.**

**My Soul's:**     **Yes, each and every human being is made up of bones, muscle, hair, genes, chromosomes, nerves, chemicals, and more. Then there is the mysterious quality that is described as "spirit" or "soul"—the nonmaterial force that goes beyond all the other elements in this phenomenal creature called a human being.**

                     **I know I am a "soul." And I recognize that this part of me comes alive and takes control when I am engaging in an activity called "prayer."**

**Adventure:**    **Prayer has been, for my soul, an adventure— planning a trip before I can be sure where the**

road will lead, what problems I will have to face and manage, or whom I will meet unplanned on the journey.

*Adventuring* is choosing the excitement that comes with risk taking and knowing that the greatest risk is to choose to avoid all risk. Yes, the greatest risk is to pass up all options, abort all possibilities, and reject all positive alternatives that promise or even imply risk.

*Adventuring* is choosing to trade:

**Security for service**

**Boredom for excitement**

**Safe isolation for involvement in positive relationships**

*Adventuring* is indulging the instinctive human compulsion to risk. The Bible calls it *faith*.

With God:    A risk-taking adventure would be reckless and irresponsible without the right relationships. Adventure is only sensible when we are well connected. Without connecting with a "North Star," we would be lost at sea, without direction, subject to whatever current, swell, or storm we encountered.

Early in my childhood I chose to relate to and "connect" with God and live in His world of faith. I was not quite five years old when I stepped into this world that awaits anyone who dares to take a chance. It is the world of faith. I have called it "Possibility Thinking."

ॐ

Are you living your soul's adventure with God through prayer? Perhaps you have chosen to steer clear of this confusing world of the soul's pilgrimage, which is often replete with contradictions, confrontations, and confusion.

I challenge you—if you haven't already done so—to step into this world called "prayer."

Yes, there are steps, rules, and universal principles that must be recognized and respected if you choose this adventurous trip. Failure to follow the signals can lead to futility, failure, and frustration. That is why I now share the sometimes subtle, unnoticed seven "levels" in this process called prayer.

After many years of experimenting and learning, I believe prayer lives itself out on at least seven levels. I've dedicated a section in this book to each one. And each level leads onward, upward, higher!

*Level One:* I call this one "I Have a Dream . . . What a Daring Adventure!" There really is no true prayer without this step. This is the early longing of the soul. Some might call it vision, or positive thinking, or even faith. The human being, unlike any other of God's creatures, has the ability to imagine and long for a different reality—to *dream!* Many powerful Possibility Thinkers who would not call this mental exercise "prayer" are practicing prayer more than they realize.

*Level Two:* This one I call "I Need Help—from Someone, Somewhere!" It is the cry of desperation, often a pitiful plea for intervention by a higher power. Repentance occurs on this level. It's a part of this process called prayer too. Is a "Help!" prayer selfish and self-centered? We'll see. Salvation is, for sure, self-centered too.

*Level Three:* "I Really Care about You!" This is the instinctive, intuitive, truly selfless reaching out to help the lost and the hurting. Another word for it is *intercession,* asking God to intercede or intervene. At this level prayer rises to high, noble, honorable, even heroic heights. The aura of altruism lingers on this level.

*Level Four:* I call this step "God, Let's Connect." Here the desire is not just to talk to God, but to listen to Him as well. Here the agenda is only to become the person God wants you to be. This is "two-way prayer," real communication. At this level you want to be responsible, you dare to become accountable to the Source and Force who gave you life before you asked for it. Level Four touches the themes of wholeness and holiness.

*Level Five:* I label this "I'm Quiet—and I'm Listening." "Meditation" also aptly describes it. Angels in heaven applaud you when you reach this point. Level Five often follows Level Four—but sometimes precedes it. Meditation has a rich history among saints of all ages, but in more recent times it has gotten a "bad rap" with, of all people, some Christians! Is that right? We'll find out.

*Level Six:* "Alleluia—Anyway!" Prayer has reached a heroic level. This one's in a class by itself. It is reserved for the heart that cannot hold back gratitude. Surprisingly, it's the level where we must go— swiftly—when tragedy strikes! Praise and thanksgiving are the humble and happy habits of those who are effervescent in their worship or anguishing in agony.

*Level Seven:* "Make Me a Blessing!" At this stage you will be an answer to someone's prayer. Your life will become a blessing. You will impulsively become a person whose prayers heal and bless those who come into your spiritual circle. Embark on this trip with God, and your life will end up here. Blessed! To be a blessing! This is prayer on the highest, holiest level!

Now, I must say clearly that prayer is mysterious and multidimensional. Who could possibly understand and explain all of what it means to communicate with the almighty, eternal God? Not I!

The seven levels I use in this book should be seen as a guide, that's all, nothing more or less. And, if you're like me, you will go back and forth among the levels during one brief prayer.

Take a trip with me. Let me, an experienced guide who is still mapping the landscape on this wonderful adventure called prayer, escort you.

With "grace-full" gratitude I say that my life has been fantastic! Incredibly fulfilling! And this simply is my life's story, as honestly as I can tell it.

Many—if not most—of the stories I relate in this book have been told before, either in my messages or my writings. But I have *never* shared in such detail the "behind-the-scenes" perspective of how prayer has impacted every critical moment of my wonderful journey with God.

I have chosen not to relate a number of important events, as well as strategic encounters with people who are near and dear to me, because my goal here is not to tell all of my life story, but to use key, memorable moments to illustrate the principles of effective prayer. I'm not preaching here—I'm witnessing. This book is not a sermon—it is my testimony.

It is my witness, under solemn oath, that prayer—*real prayer*—will lead your soul on an adventure that moves from level to level, until you hear and feel the heartbeat of my hero—the greatest adventurer of all time: Jesus.

Are you ready for the adventure?

LEVEL 1

# I HAVE A DREAM... WHAT A DARING ADVENTURE!

*I'm dreaming God's impossible dream . . . that's prayer!*

"CALL TO ME, AND I WILL ANSWER YOU, AND SHOW YOU GREAT
AND MIGHTY THINGS, WHICH YOU DO NOT KNOW."
— JEREMIAH 33:3 —

# Chapter 1

## Possibilities—They're All around You

To pray, you must first believe that some One might hear your prayer and respond favorably. Prayer is all about possibilities. About dreams. About faith.

This was the first prayer I said aloud. Like so many other children, I was taught:

*Now I lay me down to sleep,*
*I pray the Lord my soul to keep*
*If I should die before I wake,*
*I pray the Lord my soul to take. Amen.*

I memorized this prayer and said it on my knees every night beginning at the age of three.

But it was not really *my* first prayer. *My* first prayer was when I added this line: "And make me a preacher when I grow up." I was just four years and eleven months old when I prayed that simple and sincere sentence.

My Uncle Henry, a missionary, had returned to America from China and met, for the first time, his older sister's youngest child waiting at the gate. He ran up to me, ruffled my hair, and welcomed me with this enthusiastic announcement: "So you're Robert? You're going to be a preacher when you grow up!"

That moment I was launched into my soul's adventure with God.

Hours later, on my knees, I prayed *my* first prayer. No one taught me to say it. I was not coached. I freely, privately, chose the words: "And make me a preacher when I grow up." My lifetime decision was made then and there. God called me before I could be motivated by ego, fame, or fortune.

I honestly cannot recall a single night in the next twenty years that I did not repeat that simple, short, sincere prayer.

So I became a decision maker at the age of four years and eleven months! In that childhood prayer, I made a private, personal decision. I asserted leadership over the life of Robert H. Schuller. I became an optimist. The seed was planted. Although my young mind, through the words of the prayer, expressed the reality of death, "If I should die before I wake," hope got the last word: *"Make me a preacher when I grow up!"*

Without realizing it, I became a Possibility Thinker. I made a decision before I understood all the problems I would have to face.

Later, Uncle Henry filled in the details. He told me that to become a minister in our three-hundred-year-old Protestant denomination, The Dutch Reformed Church in America, I would be required by church law to finish not only high school and four years of college, but I would also have to attend postgraduate school for an additional three years to obtain a graduate theological degree.

I hadn't even started first grade yet! So at the age of four I set my first twenty-year goal when I prayed, "God make me a preacher when I grow up."

Now, more than sixty years later, I can see what really happened to that little boy in overalls. He made his first personal, private connection with the God who created him. A relationship was begun between the two of them. His personal, private, intimate soul had begun a life of adventuring with God!

## Where Would This Path Lead Me?

May 1991. I am coming down the elevator of a prominent Washington, D.C., hotel. I'm excited and honored. I've just been elected a member of the Horatio Alger organization.

I check the mirror and adjust my black tie. The tux fits great. The door opens, and I join a line entering the dining room. Many of the Horatio Alger members are familiar and famous. But I don't recognize the face of the man who turns, extends a warm hand, beams a bright smile, and greets me: "Dr. Schuller! Welcome to the club. I have watched your television program for years."

Then he politely introduces himself: "I'm Don Keough, President of Coca-Cola."

I'm impressed.

He continues, "You know, Dr. Schuller, I think we're the same age."

"I was born in 1926," I offer.

"So was I!" he responds.

"What month?" I probe.

"September."

"September? So was I!"

"What day?" I ask.

"The fourth." Now he was as curious as I.

"I was born on the sixteenth!"

"What state were you born in?" I question.

"Iowa," he says with pride.

"By golly! So was I!"

"What city?" I ask, suspecting that it must have been a prominent city, like Des Moines.

"Oh," he says with a laugh, "I was born on a small farm near a town you never heard of."

"Try me," I challenge, remembering that in Iowa they say if it's thirty-five miles away you may never have heard of it. His answer blows me away.

"Carnes."

"Carnes!" It was only eight miles from Alton, my hometown. "Did your family attend church?" I feel quite confident of this one. Nearly every Iowan was a churchgoer in those days.

"Yes. Roman Catholic. How about yours?"

"Dutch Reformed."

We stop. Joined in surprise.

In September of 1926, two baby boys were born to two Christian farm families only eight miles and twelve days apart.

Both were conceived by and born to God-fearing parents.

Both would be raised in the humblest of homes.

Both would be linked by a powerful belief in prayer.

Both would be taken on extraordinary life journeys before they would meet for the first time some sixty years later as members of an exclusive American honorary organization.

When we reach out to God in prayer, like I did on my knees beside my childhood bed, seeking to grasp great possibilities, none of us knows where the road will lead or just how it might end. But by faith, large or small, we assume and then choose to believe some One is listening! Some One who was dreaming a beautiful dream—long before He gave it to us to become our dream.

# Dreaming on the Riverbank

I never asked to be born. I was never given the opportunity to choose my parents. I had no choice over my genes. I didn't select my Uncle Henry to be my uncle. I was not given the freedom to approve or disapprove of the man who would be my father and the woman who would be my mother. And the times into which I was born were not of my making or my choosing.

The times?

World War I had ended eight years before I was born.

A new movement called communism was only eight years old in its takeover of Russia.

Versailles had crushed the once proud nation of Germany. Smashed, humiliated, battered, and beaten, the nation that boasted some of the world's greatest classical musicians, philosophers, scientists, and theologians had seen the last of its national pride bleached and battered with shame.

History would not settle for that. The collective, squelched self-esteem of the German nation would so distort its hunger for a respectable return to glory that even good people—educated persons—would stumble and be blinded by an insatiable appetite for a recovered national honor until they would follow the false promises of a fascist regime.

Hitler and Stalin would dominate the twentieth century.

But as a boy, I had no inkling of these world-shaking forces and events. My world was safe, serene, secure, and rich with solitude. I was the fifth and final child born into that poor Dutch farmer's family, following by seven years my four older siblings—one brother and three sisters.

So I grew up alone. My brothers and sisters did their assigned chores. I was left free to walk alone to the quiet river that ran through our land.

I would stand in my solitude on the hills by the river, preaching to an imaginary congregation, imitating the sounds and gestures of a seasoned preacher.

I would sit in sacred silence on the riverbank, watching white clouds slide through the soundless sea of space.

And I would dream. Of my future. Of the twenty years that lay ahead to work and wait until I would finish my formal education and be licensed by my denomination to do what I wanted to do *now*— preach!

But for now I had to wait. I had to learn one of the most powerful, possibility-producing lessons of my life—a lesson that would shape my character from childhood through adulthood. In psychology courses at Hope College, I learned that psychologists had a term for the lesson I had learned; they called it "delayed gratification."

This lesson helped me to deal with my sexuality, which would emerge in my adolescent years. When I first felt those strange signals, I shared my private feelings secretly with my father, who broke out in loud laughter I had never heard from him before.

"It only means you're healthy, son. But wait until you're married and enjoy your honeymoon."

## Never Turn Problems into Excuses

I was a happy, healthy, hopeful child. But I had a problem. I was fat. When the two sides for softball chose their players on the lawn outside the one-room schoolhouse (a school that had seventeen students in eight grades, all taught by one teacher) I was chosen last, if at all. This rejection by my peers planted seeds of low self-esteem, I'm sure.

But I compensated by being the "best preacher" in school.

"I want to learn a poem for Christmas," I told my first-grade teacher one day. "I have to learn how to speak alone on stage."

I got the part. One cold winter's night, dressed up in my Sunday suit, I delivered the poem with gusto—to the delight and applause of my beaming parents and schoolmates. In this arena, my obesity didn't seem to cause me ridicule. I learned that I could excel in the areas God had gifted me.

Our farm was another locale for valuable life lessons. I had a childhood chore. At the age of five I was assigned two cows to milk every day. Every cow in our registered herd of Ayrshires had to be milked every morning and every evening. No matter what!

Rain. Storms. Blizzards raging in subzero temperatures. The cows had to be milked—*every day!*

I hated farming! I was repelled by the barnyard smells. I recoiled at the daily drudgery. I became a lazy farm boy.

"I hope you'll be able to make a living with your mouth, because you'll never make it as a farmer," my only brother, ten years older than I, said to me after I failed to help with some farm chores.

But I was never allowed to be excused from what I and only I had to do—milk the cows assigned to me. Come what may, the cows had to be milked.

Against my will, but to my lifetime credit, I would have an invaluable quality etched deeply and permanently into my childhood character: *Painful* (Yes! My ears froze in twenty-below-zero storms) *problems are never to become excuses for quitting.*

Years later I would preach a sermon to millions of Possibility Thinkers: "Never turn problems into excuses."

So in every way—every day—God was answering my nightly prayer: "God, make me a preacher when I grow up."

What an adventure my soul was experiencing with God!

I remember my father's tears at the breakfast table the morning I excitedly told him and Mamma, "I added something to my prayer last night. I asked God to make me a preacher when I grow up." My announcement came the day after Uncle Henry's prophetic greeting.

"Why are you crying?" I asked.

Dad didn't say a word. He just cried.

"And Uncle Henry said my name is Robert. Why do you call me Harold?"

Mom answered that one. "Your grandmother wanted me to name you Robert. I wanted to name you Harold. So we named you Robert Harold. Grandma had her way. But I had my way too." She and Dad laughed.

"You were an answer to my prayers, Harold," Dad said, drying his tears.

I didn't think to ask him to explain, but later in my life I would understand his tears.

High school came. I performed in the plays. God wanted me to learn some drama.

I memorized passages by great English writers. Shakespeare. Tennyson. Browning. During my teens, I was being mentally conditioned by brilliant lines of poetry and literature.

I learned one poem I've never forgotten:

*Abou Ben Adhem (may his tribe increase!)*
*Awoke one night from a deep dream of peace,*
*And saw, within the moonlight in his room,*
*Making it rich, and like a lily in bloom,*
*An angel writing in a book of gold:—*
*Exceeding peace had made Ben Adhem bold,*
*And to the presence in the room he said,*
    *"What writest thou?"—The vision raised its head,*
*And with a look made of all sweet accord,*
*Answered, "The names of those who love the Lord."*
*"And is mine one?" said Abou. "Nay, not so,"*
*Replied the angel. Abou spoke more low,*
*But cheerily still; and said, "I pray thee, then,*

*Write me as one that loves his fellow men."*
  *The angel wrote, and vanished. The next night*
*It came again with a great wakening light,*
*And showed the names whom love of God had blest,*
*And lo! Ben Adhem's name led all the rest.*

*(James Leigh Hunt, 1834)*

ॐ

High school shaped me more than I knew. I sang in the high school quartet. We were good. We won first place in the state contest and went on to the national tournament. I enjoyed quartet singing—so much so that I tried out in college and made it.

That quartet, The Arcadian Four, did so well that we were selected for a summer concert tour to California. I fell in love with the mountains. The ocean. Palm trees.

"Lord, here's where I want to be a minister," I prayed. I now see it was God putting the "want to" in my heart to guide me!

Years later, my mentor, Raymond Beckering, answering my questions about California, said, "Yes, it's beautiful, but there just aren't any great churches there."

*Then I'll go and make one,* I dreamed! Now decades later, I see it: The dream was a prayer, for prayer is connecting with God, and God and I were "connected" in a dream!

## Learning Life-Impacting Lessons

Finally, high school was finished, and I was off to college. Hope College in Michigan.

My world was widening. History. Psychology. Debates. Oratory. Speech. God was shaping me.

Then came seminary, where I would be impacted by the first question of the Heidelberg Catechism: "What is your only comfort in life and death?"

With basic psychology fresh in my mind, I suddenly focused on what would become a life passion: using psychology and theology to bring comfort to hurting hearts.

I learned and was overwhelmed by another significant theological point in seminary: the ultimate solution to the problems of guilt and sin that infect humanity. It was in a course with the sober title "Theories of Atonement."

An important question demanded an answer: How can God be merciful and also just? Later in life I would refer to this as the ultimate contradiction. My prayer life would demand an explanation, or I'd be talking to a God that is an unresolved contradiction.

My theology professors answered, "God's justice demands that all wrongdoings be justly punished. To do less would make God immoral—a silent partner with sin and evil. But God's love demands that all sin and evil be afforded the possibility of forgiveness—or He would lack mercy and be unholy in love."

So God faced the divine dilemma—a holy contradiction. He decided to pay the punitive damages Himself. He would "take the rap" for us. Sin would be punished. He would then be truly just. Being totally innocent of human sin, He would "earn the right" to extend His mercy to all who asked for it.

He would come to earth in the life of His Son, the most beautiful person who ever lived—my hero, Jesus Christ. He would sacrifice His only Son on the ultimate altar—the cross. And there He would declare that even the worst of sins—crucifying Jesus—could be forgiven.

Jesus would end His life with the words, "Forgive them, for they know not what they do."

Years later, in an unpublished book entitled "Life's Contradictions," I wrote: "The ultimate philosophical contradiction is between mercy and justice." One chapter I titled "The Cross—A Creative Solution to the Ultimate Contradiction."

It dawned on me that as a pastor I would be a messenger of incredibly good news! God really does love, in spite of what people "do" or "don't do." If a holy, perfect, merciful, just, loving God can forgive the worst sin ever committed, then nothing is impossible with Him.

A final, life-impacting, frightening experience happened the last year of my first "twenty-year plan." I watched graduating seniors at my seminary fall into the throes of the green-eyed monster called jealousy. Each wanted the biggest and best church. But there weren't many large churches in our tiny denomination.

The largest was the Marble Collegiate Church in New York City, but Dr. Norman Vincent Peale had a lifetime lock on that job. I heard jealous young preachers criticize him. As the time of my graduation drew near, I became fearful about my own secret ambitions. Was I, at such a young age, ego driven? That thought scared me. I wanted to be immunized against jealousy. I wanted the biggest and best church, too, when my time came. God alone knows how I prayed this potentially demonic problem through.

His answer was miraculous and unexpected. How often this has been true on my soul's adventure!

"Bob Schuller." It was my professor of preaching calling out my name. "You have to turn in a paper on a great American preacher. You had a choice. You've not turned it in, so I'm giving you a name— George Truett."

I'd never heard of George Truett! Yet weeks later my whole future as a preacher would be on a fantastic lifetime track all because of this class assignment.

I learned that George Truett came as a young minister to a tiny handful of people. He started with a promise to spend his whole life with these folks and to never, ever look for, ask for, pray for, or long for a larger church.

Forty years later he would look back to see that this little church had become the largest Baptist church in the whole world—First Baptist Church in Dallas, Texas.

"God, give me a chance to go anywhere—start with nothing if you wish—and let me spend forty years building a great church for Jesus Christ!" was my new prayer.

So, just as my first twenty-year goal was achieved, I found a new forty-year goal!

Seminary ended. Dad came from Iowa to see me in cap and gown, graduating from my three years of graduate studies.

I was ordained as a preacher in the oldest Protestant denomination in the history of the United States.

And my dad cried.

Finally, twenty years later, he told me why he had cried that morning years ago when I had first told him, "I prayed last night, 'Make me a preacher when I grow up.'"

"Harold, I wanted to be a minister for Jesus Christ when I was a little boy. But my dad and mom died when I was in the sixth grade. I had to quit school and get a job as a farm hand. So I prayed, 'God, make me a minister through one of my sons someday.'

"My first baby was a girl, my second, a boy. He never liked books or school and was destined to be a farmer. The next child was a girl. And the next—our last, we thought—was a girl.

"Many years later your mom got pregnant again. It was a boy. You were born. How I prayed, 'Take him, Lord, and make him Your preacher.' But I never, never, never wanted you to know how I felt. It had to be an honest call from the Lord.

"That's why I cried when you told me, 'I'm going to be a preacher when I grow up.' God has answered my childhood prayer, Harold."

We cried and hugged.

Then I said, "But my name is Robert."

Our tears were swept away by laughter.

My soul was off and away on a lifetime adventure with God!

# Chapter 2

# Any Mountain
# Can Be Moved

If you were God and wanted to "connect" with a human being who is spiritually designed and mentally engineered to be a creative communicator, how would you approach a person who may not even be a believer?

By giving this person a vision—a dream—a hope? I believe that our hopes and dreams are the primal connection between the sacred and the secular. On this first level of prayer, the dreamer is preparing his mental soil for positive prayer.

You could call "dreaming the impossible dream" the conception of the prayer impulse. The soul is being prepared for the seeds that will sprout and blossom in prayer's passion, purpose, and power.

So listen, quietly and respectfully, when some positive-thinking person shares his hopes and dreams. He may unknowingly be under the creative influence of divine inspiration. God may be making contact: "For it is God who works in you to will and to act according to his good purpose" (Phil. 2:13, NIV).

Here's what I've learned about making great dreams come true: The dreaming of a beautiful dream is embryonic prayer.

## Mustard-Seed Faith Moves Mountains

Real prayer begins before the seeds of prayer are even planted. The spiritual soil for fruit-bearing prayer must be prepared for seeding.

I grew up on an Iowa farm. To me, farming is a paradigm of prayer.

When does the farmer begin the process of farming? When he plants the first seed? No! The first stage is the careful readying of the ground. The dry crust must be plowed. The plowed chunks then must be broken up. The churned soil then must be raked smooth and soft until it is receptive to the planting of the seed. Seeding is the second stage in the process.

The first step of the process called prayer is the opening of a sealed mind to envision and respectfully receive a positive possibility.

Prayer begins with hope: "There must be something more." Prayer is reaching beyond your grasp. As Robert Browning wrote, "A man's reach must exceed his grasp, or what's a heaven for?" Prayer is dreaming a dream until it consumes you!

My witness is this: Positive thinking and Possibility Thinking are what the Bible calls *faith*.

And basic faith is Level One in the process called prayer.

This explains why faith "moves mountains." Think of all the promises of Christ that inspire us to believe that nothing is impossible with God. He says, "If you have faith as a mustard seed, you will say to this mountain, 'Move from here to there,' and it will move; and nothing will be impossible for you" (Matt. 17:20).

Christ never said the mountain would be *removed*. But He did promise that the mountain would *move*. *Every mountain I've ever faced*—and there have been a few—*has moved when I prayed on the positive-thinking level.*

"But your daughter's leg was amputated, Dr. Schuller," an angry, cynical person once said to me. He was accusing me of spiritual hypocrisy. "Faith didn't grow a new leg. The mountain didn't go away!"

I had quoted the Scripture, "Prayer changes things," and this upset him.

"Possibility Thinking is prayer at the first level," I answered. "It is positive faith reaching out for a positive reaction to a challenging reality. And miracles do happen."

In every case where I've faced a mountain and prayed in faith, my perception of the problem was altered. My soul saw a vision:

God would allow the scar to be turned into a star. Prayer on the Possibility-Thinking level gave me a vision of how God could turn

Tragedy into triumph,

Hurts into halos,

Pain into gain,

Stumbling blocks into stepping stones,

Obstacles into opportunities,

Difficulties into dividends,

Mountains into miracles.

*Always,* positive prayer changed my perception of the mountain! Then the miracle happened. Deep inside my suffering soul, it happened. The mountain moved. It changed from an enemy inflicting evil into a friend promising me blessings from my burdens. Bad luck turned into good luck. Always!

One of my dear friends, John Wimber, founder of Vineyard Ministries, was struck with cancer. His first words to the public who helped pray him through the suffering were, "The view from the valley is not too bad."

# The Mountain Got Smaller!

I was in my early twenties when the tornado roared out of the quiet Iowa twilight. With the distant hum like freight trains roaring fast upon us, we escaped with our lives.

Our family became homeless.

We were crushed. With a huge mortgage due on the farm and the Great Depression still a fresh memory, my father wept when he saw the dead cattle, shards of lumber stuck in their lifeless bodies like toothpicks in olives.

The country church was packed the next night as farmers came to pray for those who had lost everything. Correction. Not *everything*.

The wiped-out farmers, with broken hearts and dashed dreams, still held on to a mustard-seed-sized kernel of faith. How they prayed. The country church was so quiet you could hear muffled sniffles as the elders and deacons rose one by one to pray.

A young boy, a student studying to be a preacher, stood to pray. He had come home only two days before for summer vacation.

His soul sobbed. His lips opened.

He prayed, remembering the words of William Cowper:

*God moves in a mysterious way*
*His wonders to perform;*
*He plants His footsteps in the sea*
*And rides upon the storm.*

It was my first public prayer—in tears—in my childhood church. The mountain moved. *It got smaller while our faith grew bigger.*

We looked back on the "total loss" of our lives: Cattle and machinery—all gone. We would later say, "If it hadn't been for that tornado, Dad might well have had his farm foreclosed when the mortgage fell due two months later."

The morning after that sad prayer meeting, the insurance agent called: "You didn't have much insurance, Tony. All you'll get is three thousand dollars."

My dad, verbalizing a "Level One" prayer that brimmed with faith, said, "That's okay. We'll make it. We're homeless, but we can sleep in my married daughter's home. We'll build another little house."

We did. For months there had been a sign on an old house in town. It read, "For sale. $50.00 if removed from the site."

We spent the first fifty dollars of the three thousand dollars insurance money. We bought the old house, took it apart board by board, nail by nail, and hauled it on a wagon to the farm. It was all we would need to build a new—but tiny—home.

There my dad and I, with hammer and saw, built a new house.

My dad took the remaining $2,950 to the bank, saying, "I want to make a payment on the mortgage. I can't pay all of it. But I'll pay $2,950 of it."

I watched the proud banker's eyes fill with tears as he said, "Tony! That's great! That's enough to allow me to refinance the loan. We'll rewrite the terms for another twenty years!" This saved our farm.

But what about me? Could I go back to school? Or would I have to drop out and get a job?

That negative thought never controlled my mind for one moment. Our hopes and our hurts became a prayer! God was still faithfully answering a little boy's prayer: "Make me a preacher when I grow up."

Disappointed? Yes—a tornado will do that to you. Discouraged and depressed? No—that is something only we can do to ourselves!

I returned to school and found a job as a janitor, cleaning toilets in the Women's Club building three blocks from the seminary. After my classes in Bible, Greek, Hebrew, and preaching, I would go to work. It was a good job, when "jobs couldn't be found."

I discovered that even in the hardest times there are a few jobs nobody wants. Dirty. Low paying. But it was an answer to prayer for me.

I couldn't eat well on the few dollars I earned, so I lived on sweet rolls, chocolate bars, and milk. My diet was unhealthy, and I broke out in horrible pimples. Not good.

I would develop a problem called *rhinophyma*. My slim nose began to swell. Blue. Purple. Worse and worse it became. Radiation therapy at Mayo Brothers didn't work. A young preacher's face was distorted by a distracting and dangerous "W. C. Fields" nose.

"Surgery is your only hope," the doctor said. I would have several plastic surgeries in order to have a normal nose again. Another scar God turned into a star.

I continued to work hard and thanked God, who was still answering my childhood prayer.

World War II was raging when the tornado wiped us out. Farm prices escalated. Crops were great. Our farm was paid for in ten years. When he retired, my dad bought a comfortable house in Alton, Iowa, for which he paid cash. No more mortgages! He lived and died there a happy and prosperous man. The mountain moved.

God was preparing me to be a preacher with a soul soaked in this biblical promise: "All things work together for good to those who love God, to those who are the called according to His purpose" (Rom. 8:28).

After the tornado came the fire in my college dormitory. Another mountain. Everything in my rooming house was turned to ashes. I was homeless—for a second time.

In the fire I lost my English term paper, and it was too near the end of the semester to do it over. I got my first F on a report card. But I was not dropped from school.

"Bob," the professor said, "this is not a required course for graduates. But let me advise you to forget writing in your life. Focus on public speaking, not on being an author."

I prayed. The years rolled on. This is my thirtieth book.

The mountain moved.

## My Problem Led to a Miracle

Another mountain moved.

One of the most memorable miracles of my lifetime grew out of one of the most perilous mountains I ever faced.

I will never, ever doubt that I experienced a miracle.

I was overweight by at least fifty pounds at the age of twenty-five. I went to the doctor, and he taught me a word I had never heard in my home: *calories.*

"Four thousand calories equal one pound, coming and going," he explained. "Eat four thousand more calories than your body burns, and you will gain a pound. On the other hand, if your body burns four thousand more calories than you've consumed, then you will lose a pound."

"You," the doctor told me, "use up about 2,500 calories a day at your age and activity level. I'll put you on a 1,500-calorie-a-day diet. That means you'll earn 1,000 calories a day toward weight loss. In four days that's 4,000 calories, and you'll lose a pound. Stay with it and you'll lose two pounds every eight days."

Then he told me the calories in foods. I couldn't believe it! Four hundred calories in one sweet roll! Fifty calories in a butter slice! Three hundred calories in a chocolate-covered doughnut! Five hundred calories in a malted milk! Almost none in celery, carrots, strawberries, tomatoes, lettuce, and cabbage.

I listened. I learned. I lived with the new plan. And I lost fifty pounds in five months.

But gradually, over the years, I regained the weight.

My suits became too tight. Finally I bought a new suit. Boy, it felt good! The new suit was two sizes larger. I didn't "feel overweight" now. I had room to grow. So I continued to gain weight.

I could see what was happening. I battled it at the table and on my knees. No answer.

It was my problem. "Yes, this is your problem, Bob," was the only subtle signal I could pick up.

But God was setting me up for a miracle.

One unforgettable day I made a trip to Florida. My aide and I traveled together. "It's time for me to quit kidding myself," I said to him. "I'm fat. So starting tonight at dinner I'm going to watch what I eat and consume no more than fifteen hundred calories a day."

We were greeted at the airport, taken to our hotel, and then to dinner.

"This is one of the best restaurants in America," my host proudly told me. He showed me the menu.

I ordered salad with loads of cheese—400 calories worth. I ordered steak—marbleized—700 calories. A baked potato—150 calories, plus 300 calories of sour cream! The bread was fantastic. I ate three slices—with butter. Another 400 calories.

"Key lime pie," the host said. "It's a Florida specialty."

I had never tried it. So I ordered a slice—another 500 calories. I was stuffed.

I went to my room and prepared for bed. I was ridden with guilt. I felt hopeless.

I remember lying on my back, arms flat at my sides, palms open, feet apart. I prayed.

"Jesus? Can you help me? I'm totally helpless."

I fell asleep.

Suddenly in the middle of the night I awakened. No touch. No personal presence of God. But something I've never experienced before or since. I had a vision.

It was like watching a movie. I saw a river like the one that ran through my childhood farm. The quiet, narrow stream was now flooded beyond its banks. The little brook was almost a quarter-mile wide! It reached to the top of the hill where I sat. Here the floodwaters were deceptively gentle, flowing over the green, grassy pasture. The water near me appeared so harmless and safe. But farther out, in the center of the river, the water rushed wild, in racing waves. There in the middle of that torrential current I could see it—a large uprooted tree, roots white, being carried away! Dead. Destroyed.

The application was clear. I saw that my body was that uprooted tree. The gentle water close to me was a cruel deception. The thick slice of steak, the cheese, the pie, the buttery bread—all were so seemingly innocent. But they were uprooting my health the way the high flood-waters had uprooted the tree. I was being destroyed by "good" things.

Then this message came from Jesus Christ in words that flashed through my mind: "I have snatched you from destruction."

Instantly I knew I was saved from wanting the good tasting but harmful foods. I was dramatically delivered in a momentous, mysterious, miraculous visitation! I was overwhelmed by a peace I can only define as the presence of Jesus Christ coming to answer my prayer. I fell asleep.

On the trip home my appetite and desire for high-calorie foods was gone! I couldn't touch them. I was not being deprived. I was not on a diet. My taste had been totally altered.

Now I loved salad and fresh fruit. In a matter of four months, with no willpower of my own, I lost forty pounds.

That was twenty years ago. My eating habits remain the same today. I have been "snatched from destruction."

## God Was Just Getting Started with Me

Only two months after the miracle in Florida, Walt Frederick, a member of my church who had noticed my battle with the bulge called on me. "I've been praying for you, pastor, and the Lord has told me I have to help you with your weight problem," he said.

I told him about my miracle in Florida.

"But He has something else to tell you, and I've been asked to help you."

I listened.

"You must get on an exercise program. I am a Boston Marathon runner. I am going to be your trainer. Follow me. Now."

"Now?"

"Yes, now."

He led me outdoors. He was in stylish sweats; I was in a suit, black socks, and oxfords.

"We'll walk," he said. We walked one block. Two blocks.

"Stop," he said. "See this light pole? See the next one? We'll jog very slowly, but we'll trot from this pole to the next."

We jogged.

I puffed.

We walked three more blocks. Again he stopped. "Let's try once more, running from this light pole to the next."

We did.

"Good!" he said. "Good! Now I'll see you again on Friday, and I'll bring a pair of running shoes for you. What size are you?"

"Ten and a half," I answered. "But, Friday! I'm getting ready to go to Japan on Sunday!"

He turned, locked his eyes with mine, and spoke. "Is going to Japan more important than saving your body? Pastor Bob, the Lord has told me He has great plans for you, and your physical health is all important. Listen to me! Or you'll die too young!"

I grumbled, but I heard my friend Walt loud and clear. With his encouragement, I started a running program long before it was the "in" thing to do. I have never given it up.

❧

I had a good flight to Japan. Reservations were made for me at the New Otani Hotel. I did not choose the hotel. I did not choose this speaking assignment. I did not choose the date.

I was about to have an experience I had never had before and have never had since.

God knew how easily my psychologically trained brain worked, with its critical and analytical mental habits. God was going to teach me flatly and irrevocably that what had happened in Florida only a few weeks before was a *divine* miracle. I would never question it after my Tokyo trip.

Here's how God did it.

It was late in the afternoon only a week later. I was in my Japanese hotel room with my wife, Arvella. We had a couple of free hours.

"Let's go shopping," I said. "I'd like to find a stereo set we could buy."

"Go ahead," she said. "I'm tired. I'm going to nap. There are three floors of shops beneath the ground floor of this hotel. Check them out and let me know if you find anything."

I almost objected. I was so close to saying, "Forget it. I'll take a nap too, and we'll go together tomorrow morning." Thank God I yielded instead to an impulse and said, "Okay."

I went out the door to the elevator. "What floor should I try?" I asked myself. I pressed one of the buttons and came off the elevator on one of the three underground floors. I don't recall which floor it was.

I strolled down the hall. Stores all over! Both sides! Windows filled with radios, stereos, TVs. Impulsively I picked a store and walked in. I looked at the merchandise and checked the prices—half what they would cost in America!

"What will it cost to ship it to the U.S.?" I asked the clerk.

Then another customer, whom I hadn't noticed, answered, "Why don't you check it with your airline luggage?" Before I could answer, he continued. "Are you here for the medical conference too?"

I was impressed with the man's stature, his shining black face, his colorful African turban, and his bright-colored robe that reached the floor.

"No," I answered. "I'm here for a convention, but it's not the medical convention."

"What is it?" he inquired.

"Oh," I said, "it's a religious conference."

He came alive. "Are you a Christian?" he asked.

"Yes, I am."

His eyes flashed. He reached out with both hands to grasp mine. "Thank God! I'm a Christian too! And I count it a day lost if I've not had a chance to meet another Christian!" He was beaming with a holy, heavenly light.

"Tell me, where are you from? And were you born into a Christian family?" I asked.

By now we had both forgotten where we were and why we were in the store.

"Oh no!" he answered. "My parents were not Christians. They didn't believe in God. My father, who was the chief, died, and I became the chief.

"Then I fell deathly ill. Doctors were flown in from England. The diagnosis was clear. Three doctors came in to report to me. 'Chief, we have bad news. You are dying. You do not have long to live. We must tell you so you can arrange a successor.'

"I couldn't believe it. 'What about America?' I asked. 'They must have new medicines or new treatments there.' They shook their heads.

"'No, chief. You are dying, and there is nothing or no one who can help you.'

"Then I became angry. I shouted at them, 'Then get out! Go! Get out of here!' They turned and closed the door.

"I lay flat on my bed. Dying. An atheist. No son to give my chiefdom to. Then I found myself saying, 'God, are you really there— alive—and can You heal me?'

"Instantly I had a vision. Like a movie in my mind, I saw a blanket descend from the sky. It was old, tattered, ready to fall apart if anyone touched it. Instantly I knew that blanket was my body. Then this message came *clear* and *strong* into my consciousness, 'I have healed you.' The blanket was suddenly restored to perfectly new cloth!

"I knew, I just knew it was the Lord! I knew nothing, I mean *nothing,* about God or Jesus. I called the nurse. 'I must find a mission-ary and call the doctors back.'

" 'We have no idea what could have happened,' they said. 'I am a Christian,' one of them said. 'I didn't want to offend your belief that there is no God, so I didn't tell you. But I prayed as I left this room, and my prayer was answered! You have been visited by God. You have been healed.' "

The incredible parallelism between his miracle in Nigeria and mine in Florida were beyond human contrivance.

What were the odds of our meeting? In another country? In the *same hotel,* the *same store,* on the *same floor,* at the *same moment,* with the *same kind of story?*

"I wanted you to know and never question my visit to you in Florida," was the message I got then and there from God—never, ever to be doubted or forgotten in my skeptical mind!

"More things are wrought by prayer than this world dreams of."

What an amazing, miraculous, adventure my soul has been on with my God.

# Dream the Impossible Dream

My point is so simple. *There's power in prayer.* And the powerful beginning of prayer is faith. Norman Vincent Peale called it positive thinking.

How many people fail to connect with the Power behind prayer because they jump right in on Level Two? They cry "Help!" before they "dream." Yes, the proper preparation of the soul's soil for planting the seeds of prayer is to first condition the soul with dynamic, Possibility-Thinking faith.

Positive thinking is Level One in the prayer process. Yes, "faith conditioning" is the preparatory step in real prayer.

It's like physical exercise. "Why do I have to stretch?" I once challenged my physical fitness trainer. "I want to *exercise.* Build my lungs! Strengthen my heart! Tone my muscles! Stretching my muscles isn't exercising."

But my trainer won the argument. "You can injure your muscles if you don't stretch them, carefully, slowly, faithfully," he explained. I was paying him. That's the only reason I listened.

Months later—now years later—I came to see how right he was.

It's a universal principle—in farming, in exercising, in prayer: The first step in the process is getting ready for the real thing!

Choose to believe! Decide to become a believer, and you're already setting out on the wonderful adventure called prayer and opening your mind to dream a beautiful, God-inspired dream.

Move in slowly, respectfully, and reverently. And you'll be exercising real, redemptive repentance. For what is repentance? It's not self-condemnation; it's personal regeneration. It's turning out of darkness into light.

The Greeks had a word for it: *metanoia.* A creative act of moving from a sin-controlled life to a God-controlled life.

And what is sin? It's a condition before it is an action. And the condition is unbelief. Call it stubborn doubt. Call it a rejection of faith. Call it negative thinking. Call it cynical skepticism.

Real, life-generating repentance is rejecting proud doubt and turning to humble, quiet faith. Cynical doubt is arrogance. Willingness to believe is healing humility.

So, dreaming God's dream is the first positive act of repentance. Creative believing is healthy repentance.

This is Level One in the process of prayer. It's basic. "Without faith it is impossible to please him; for anyone who comes to God must believe that he exists and that he rewards those who search for him" (Heb. 11:6, NEB).

Prayer at the dreaming level of Possibility Thinking sets in motion energies more mysterious and powerful than we fully understand. It remained for medical science at the end of the twentieth century to discover that the brain, as a biological organ, secretes a healing chemical when it is stimulated by positive thoughts. All of our organs generate and release chemicals when stimulated by ideas. The brain is no exception. It injects powerful chemicals called endorphins into the biological system. Science and religion have become healing partners in the late twentieth century. Positive thinking is indeed the piercing power point of positive prayer.

I invite you to make a decision to move your mountain. Choose to have faith, and your mountain of doubt will move.

After over a half century of testing this philosophy of living, I agree with Corrie ten Boom's beautiful acrostic on FAITH:

*F*antastic
*A*dventuring
*I*n
*T*rusting
*H*im.

Yes! On Level One something has happened. Your mind has been opened through Possibility Thinking. Your mind has responded to the spiritual impulse, *There must be something more!* Your mind has moved to envision another world beyond the perceived horizon.

The imagination has sent its signals, etching and sketching the images of the outreaching heart.

Suddenly—or slowly—a vision appears.

A hope is born.

A decision is conceived.

A miracle is imagined.

A spiritual door opens to your soul.

The doubter begins to see and sense and savor *a dream*.

God has connected with your soul and is calling you to a grand adventure.

The human mind now moves beyond its own safe, sensible but limited capabilities.

Now the human hunger for hope has taken you over the secular edge into the sacred circle of a divine dream. You are leaping beyond the human realm to touch the divine level of living.

Now you must call out for "Help!" to the God who connected with you in your dream. The dream is impossible? Of course! It's God's way of setting you up to call on Him for help!

You must move beyond Level One. You are ready for Level Two—

"Help!" The mental stretching—Possibility Thinking—has plowed and broken up the hard mental soil of stubborn, negative thinking, and you are mentally prepared and liberated to ask for, experience, and accept the energy of God's help.

Music plays. Light floods the room where your soul dwells.

Possibility Thinking, which started out so simply, has stimulated and aroused hidden passions that cannot and will not be held back without giving God a chance to turn the impossible dream into a glorious adventure!

Dream the beautiful, impossible dream and you are making a "connection with God." And that is prayer on Level One!

Move up to the next step.

You are ready for Level Two: "I Need Help!"

You will need it!

You will never make it on your own! Just be "confident of this very thing, that He who has begun a good work in you will complete it" (Phil. 1:6).

# I NEED HELP—FROM SOMEONE, SOMEWHERE!

*The dream is impossible? Of course! It's God's way
of setting me up to call Him for help!*

"IF YOU HAVE FAITH AS A MUSTARD SEED, YOU WILL SAY TO THIS
MOUNTAIN, 'MOVE FROM HERE TO THERE,' AND IT WILL MOVE;
AND NOTHING WILL BE IMPOSSIBLE FOR YOU."
— MATTHEW 17:20 —

# Chapter 3

# God and I Are Connecting One-on-One

H*elp!* Help *me!"*
You have arrived at Level Two on this prayer adventure. Now you understand that to fulfill your potential or grasp the dream beyond your fingertips, you need help.

"Are You listening, God?" you ask. "And if You are there, can You—will You—help me?"

Level Two prayer is prayer on the sincere yet self-serving level. And God responds! God does hear. God does listen. God does connect. God does love. God will lead. God will make His marvelous, mysterious, and miraculous moves.

But before this next level is reached, the soul set on this adventure must deal with the very existence of *God.*

"Really, must I deal with *that?"* you may ask.

Yes, before going any further you must make the ultimate choice. You must accept or reject belief in God's existence.

Classical religious philosophy gives you these options:

**Atheism:**       **There is no God. There is no supreme being. There is no higher power. (However, atheists are *believers;* they have chosen to believe that there is no one higher than them.)**
**Agnosticism:**  **Maybe there is a God. Maybe there isn't.**

Deism:          A supreme being exists, but He doesn't interact
                with the world. God created the world and set
                life in motion. Then He let go and hasn't been
                heard from since.

Pantheism:      God is universal energy but is not a supreme in-
                telligence. He is cosmic energy, but He doesn't
                judge, love, plan, or empower. He's powerful, but
                He is not intelligent. God cannot think.

Theism:         God is an intelligent person. He's a living, loving,
                thinking, planning Master who created and still
                creates. He created a creature called a human be-
                ing, who in a limited way is endowed with the
                divine potential to be a creative thinker. You and
                I can think! We can choose. We can love. We are
                free to make decisions. We even have the mental
                power to imagine God's existence. We are persons.
                We have the innate ability to have faith. Jews,
                Muslims, Catholics, and Protestants are theists.

I was once asked, "Many people who practice positive thinking
are in the New Age religious movement, and many are pantheists. Why
aren't you?"

I answered, "I cannot choose to believe in a God who is less
than a human. Any God who cannot think, decide, and choose is *less
than a human being.* For humans can at least imagine, dream, and
love. I could not believe in a God who is *less* than a human!"

Prayer, to the theist, is more than positive thinking. It is Possibility
Thinking: *It's possible that there is a God who knows and cares about
me. Through prayer I will call out to Him.*

And God will take my call! But I have to tune in to get on His
wavelength. My receiving "dish" must face and be tuned to the satellite
before it can get the message. That's what the Bible means when it
calls for a humble, penitent spirit before I call out for help. Repentance
is tuning in; forgiveness—a healthy, static-free connection with God—
is the result.

And without true forgiveness at the deepest level, I will knowingly or unknowingly be controlled by the static-generating emotion of guilt, which creates interference in the spiritual broadcast from God to me. Real forgiveness makes for clear reception. The word *atonement* means "at-*one*-ment." God and I are connecting!

# God Loves Me Even Though I'm Not Perfect

Perhaps because I was raised in such a morally and spiritually strong family, church, and community, I was never taught "The Sinner's Prayer," the prayer many evangelists ask listeners in their audience to repeat.

My early religious training was, I believe, good. We didn't get drunk, use drugs, or steal. We were taught to live within boundaries and respect them.

Sexual promiscuity was simply not an accepted behavior. Almost all young people were virgins when they married. In our isolated rural community, we simply weren't exposed to the temptations and sins that I have seen thrown at everyone in the later decades of the twentieth century.

From earliest childhood I was taught the simple song "Jesus Loves Me, This I Know." I grew up knowing that God loved me—period. I learned and accepted grace, that God loves me even though I'm not perfect.

This remains a mystery in my soul's collection of memories: Why wasn't I more troubled by guilt?

Perhaps it was because religious training in the Dutch Reformed community had a careful listing of "sins" and sinful behavior. Both "right" and "wrong" were very clear.

It was a sin to miss church on Sunday. We always attended. It was common to see persons with five-year, ten-year, even twenty-year perfect attendance records in Sunday school.

It was a sin to fish on Sunday. Or use scissors on Sunday. Or—when radio came to our home—to listen to the radio unless the program was religious. We always listened to the Mormon radio broadcast:

choir, organ, hymns, and the spoken word. This was okay, even though we were taught not to believe in Mormonism.

It was a sin to work on Sunday, except to milk the cows and feed the pigs. Never—not once—did a farmer in our community work in his fields on Sunday.

It was a sin to use alcohol, except as medicine.

It was not a sin to smoke. Tobacco was a big thing in Holland. My grandfather smoked cigars, as did the ministers in the church. I learned how to make and smoke cigarettes made from corn silks, and I never prayed for forgiveness. Smoking simply wasn't a sin! My memory still responds positively to the smell of smoke from a pipe or a good cigar.

My life was protected by stable boundaries.

Years later I would be impressed by psychological studies in which children were observed in different playground arrangements. They were first allowed only to play in fenced areas. They would dash across the play areas, running to the fence and stopping themselves with a crash against the wire mesh. Without fear they would safely stop themselves. They freely enjoyed the whole fenced-in area.

To test the theory that "fences negatively restrict the emotional freedom of children," the fences were removed. Surprisingly, the children were more restrained. They ran hard only in the center of the play area. They moved slowly and cautiously when they approached the fenceless boundaries.

In another study, one in which railings on bridges were removed, people stayed further from the edge. When rails were erected, people freely approached the brink, even leaning on the rails to look over.

I grew up with *moral fences.* I respected them. I obeyed the rules. I avoided "sins." Thus I grew up without a strong "I am a sinner" self-image. God and I were connected! We were listening to and hearing each other.

I was taught that every person born inherits Adam's sin; every newborn baby is a sinner. That confused me. How could babies be sinners? They didn't fish on Sundays. They didn't swear.

"Their sinful nature is rebellion against God," I was taught, but I didn't understand. I couldn't see how they were rebelling against God.

Meanwhile, I was "okay." I'd been baptized as a child, which in our denomination meant I was branded as a sheep in Christ's flock. So I didn't have to be afraid of sin. I simply had to learn the rules, understand the boundaries, and obey the regulations.

I felt free within the "fences" that surrounded me. More than that—I believed in Jesus. He was my best friend. I had a relationship with Some One who loved me even though He knew me at my worst.

In college psychology I would learn about unconditional love and nonjudgmental acceptance as the basic principles for emotional, mental, and spiritual health and wholeness. I now know that God's ideas connected with His Spirit within me, which was and still is the Spirit of Jesus, who has occupied the central place in my heart of hearts from my earliest days, when I often sang,

*Jesus loves the little children,*
*All the children of the world.*
*Red and yellow, black and white,*
*They are precious in His sight—*
*Jesus loves the little children of the world.*

## A Special Relationship with Jesus Christ

Of course, I have had to deal with the burden of guilt—real guilt! As much, if not more, from sins of "omission" than from sins of "commission."

Sins of *commission*—when we commit an act that is wrong. God gave us the Ten Commandments to spare us from acts that would harm and shame Him and ourselves. He wants to be proud of His beautiful children, and He wants to be proud and not ashamed of who we are. But to focus only on sins of commission will result in a negative-thinking life filled with "don'ts."

Sins of *omission* are failures to do all the good we should do. Sins of omission? Yes, I sin by failing to do the good I could and should do!

Focus on sins of omission, and you'll ask positive questions. What could I do if I had more faith? What should I do to be the generous, good, and beautiful person God wants me to be? How often has He sent me beautiful, inspiring dreams, and I simply dismissed them because I wasn't "good enough, or smart enough, or worthy enough" to seize these dreams and make them mine!

How often was a low self-image the taproot of my sins of omission? And my experience of God's grace in forgiving me my sins of omission—did this become the powerful source and force that led me into a satisfying, safe, and sanctified theology of self-esteem?

Possibility Thinking was often the result of my guilt from the sins of omission. How? By a positive confession: "I am somebody! And I can do something!" That's *positive* repentance. I'm changing—from the darkness of impossibility thinking to the light of Possibility Thinking.

God's forgiveness would come in the form and face of a consuming passion for excellence. The drive to achieve the beautiful dream was God's way of pardoning me. I was saved—to be His servant.

And, of course, if we haven't dealt with the sins of omission, we will be set up for committing sins of commission. The person who is consumed and driven by Possibility-Thinking dreams is spared from boredom! He or she is excited! Enthused! Saved from boredom, that dangerous emptiness of heart that is an open door to carnal sins such as illicit sex or taking illegal drugs. The idle mind is "the devil's workshop."

Thank God that I never faced the heavy shame and guilt related to sinful sexuality or marital unfaithfulness, which is so pathetically pervasive today. Possibility Thinking packed my life so full with meaning I was prevented from the temptations that could have corrupted me. Moreover, pornographic magazines were a rarity in my childhood years. Back then, the closest thing to sexual pictures was found in Montgomery Ward and Sears and Roebuck catalogs, in which humans modeled underwear.

During the TV evangelist scandals, a concerned teenage member of our church wrote me a note: "Dr Schuller, I'm so glad we don't have to worry about you! You're too old!"

Guilt? Yes, I have and do experience guilt, but I find a model for repentance and comfort in Psalm 51:10–12:

CREATE IN ME A CLEAN HEART, O GOD,
AND RENEW A STEADFAST SPIRIT WITHIN ME.
DO NOT CAST ME AWAY FROM YOUR PRESENCE,
AND DO NOT TAKE YOUR HOLY SPIRIT FROM ME.
RESTORE TO ME THE JOY OF YOUR SALVATION,
AND UPHOLD ME BY YOUR GENEROUS SPIRIT.

I would pray this again and again in my adventure with God. Forgiveness! Grace! I've needed it! For . . .

- **My unhealthy eating habits**
- **My internalized anger at people who conspired against me in my ministry**
- **My treatment of people in ways that reduced or ruined their dignity**
- **My hypocrisy—preaching self-esteem but not practicing and applying it to myself and to those I lived and worked with**

But depressing confession and negative repentance have never been an overly repressing emotional force in my soul's adventure with God. Why?

- **Perhaps because I grew up experiencing moral character development in a frame of reference called "delayed gratification."**
- **Perhaps because I grew up with clearly defined fences and boundaries, and I was never tempted to violate them.**
- **Perhaps because the call to be a preacher came so early in my life. I just had no time or room in my life for immoral behavior.**

- Perhaps because "I was saved." Yes, my soul was saved from the rule and ruin of sin. I can take no credit for this. I was simply introduced to Jesus my Savior while I was sitting on the piano bench, singing hymns about Him while my mom played the piano.
- Perhaps because my goals were clearly set. I was a "goal-managed" person. I now see and sense that my goals were God inspired. So a goal-driven life is a God-guided life when God inspires the goal!

Surely, my soul from childhood had a very special love relationship with Jesus Christ.

## My Soul's Destiny Is Settled

It was a distinct, momentous, very personal and passionate event in my life when I stood, went forward, and all alone, without my friends or peers to accompany me, joined the church.

In my teen years I went to the First Reformed Church in Orange City, Iowa. The balcony was always full of adolescent boys. We were allowed to sit up there, separate from our parents who sat with the smaller children in the pews on the main floor.

We teenage boys sang the hymns. But first we put our wads of gum on the bottom of the pews. What a collection of rough, hard gum bumps I could feel there! We would sometimes giggle and whisper. But we listened to the sermons.

Dr. Henry Colenbrander preached. He shouted. He whispered.

One Sunday he announced, "The Consistory [the elders] will meet Wednesday night. If you aren't a member of the church, I invite you to come and confess your faith in Jesus Christ as your personal Savior. You cannot simply presume that you are a Christian. You have to make a decision to become a Christian. It must be your heart and soul coming to Jesus and saying, 'I accept You as my Savior, and I promise You I'll be Yours for the rest of my life. And when I die I'll trust You alone to receive me into Your heavenly home.'"

I felt the urgency of his words. I can still feel it. That Wednesday night I drove alone to the elders' meeting. I confessed my faith. I made my commitment. My soul's destiny was settled.

৵

Years later, while I was a student at Hope College, our male quartet sang for a visiting preacher. He would later become a full-time evangelist. His name was Billy Graham.

We sang. Billy preached. Then he did something I had never seen or heard any Reformed Church minister do. He asked people to step out of their seat, walk down the aisle to the front of the church, and make a commitment to accept Jesus Christ as Savior.

Once again, I wanted to do that! And in my heart I did. But I do not recall that Billy laid a heavy guilt trip on the people. He didn't have to. Deep down in our hearts, we knew we were normal human beings—imperfect persons who sinned and needed grace.

What hit me, beautifully, was the warm and wonderful opportunity to "come forward" and tell my college world that I loved Jesus Christ and wanted to live only and all for Him.

But I would soon be exposed to another view of what would be called—correctly or incorrectly—Christianity.

I would hear other preachers sermonizing to make good people feel oppressively guilty. Yes, barring sinners from the freedom to believe that real forgiveness is truly possible. Devout Christians heard preachers tell them they must stand up and repeat the sinner's prayer. Guilt was generated by the manipulation of emotions until men and women, already friends and followers of Christ, were made to feel "unsaved" and "lost" if they didn't stand up and confess and repent of their sins.

They were given, in my opinion, a polluted message of shame, humiliation, and undeserved embarrassment, all because they were not—and would never be—pure, sinless, perfect, holy, faultless individuals.

This didn't sit right with my soul. It would be the first stirring in my spirit that would lead me to study and propose "self-esteem theology"—what I believe is the biggest breakthrough in my soul's adventure with God!

## Do I Have to Forgive Everyone, Always?

I wonder, today, how my soul came to this consuming compulsion to love the Lord, myself, and others—including those of other faiths and other moral, cultural, and spiritual viewpoints. I wonder when my soul found it most difficult to love (of all people) people who call themselves Christians but whose spirit and style offend God's Spirit who is within the core of every saved soul.

For instance, after my son's divorce I found it difficult to love, *really* love, the woman who was my son's first wife. I harbor no hatred for her. I never have. And I do love her for carrying in her womb the first two children born to my son. We could not stop the divorce, and, right or wrong, I blamed her for it.

Am I still angry with her? No. I was. Especially when she sold a terribly untrue story about her father-in-law, "the television preacher," to a tabloid.

The divorce was still fresh when a tabloid that is sold in all of the supermarkets of America offered her a large sum of money for a report that was untrue, unfair, and damaging not only to me, the grandfather of her first two children, but to the entire family.

I was angry. But ten years later, she apologized in a letter to me. I accepted. Have I forgiven her? Yes. But not until she apologized. Her act of godly repentance prompted my immediate forgiveness.

My soul learned a lesson in that chapter of my life's private relationships. "Is it a sin," I asked, "not to forgive a person who has not repented of a wrongdoing?" I concluded that we are not spiritually obligated to forgive an unrepentant person who cannot claim—like the soldiers who crucified Christ—innocence by virtue of ignorance: "Father, forgive them for they know not what they do."

I was spared from guilt in not forgiving her before her repentance because of my understanding of how God treats me and all other people.

I truly believe that God does not forgive intentional sinful behavior unless and until the sinner sincerely asks for forgiveness. When sinners know they are hurting innocent people, they must be willing to turn away, with God's help, from their destructive behaviors. Finally, they must be motivated to be moved and molded by God's Spirit.

# "I'm Sorry! I'm So Sorry!"

"You've got to come, Bob!" Dr. Leon Sullivan said. "It's the second African/African-American Conference to be held in Libreville, the capitol of Gabon. You're the only white minister invited. If you don't come, there won't be a white pastor there."

There was no living black leader in the world that I admired and respected more than Leon. For years he pastored a large Baptist Church in Philadelphia. There he founded O.I.C., Opportunities Industrial Centers, where he taught unemployed African-Americans trades that lifted them from the indignity of welfare to the pride of honorable, constructive, rewarding work.

More than one million persons were now proudly employed as craftsmen, thanks to Leon and his creative and liberating ministry!

For more than thirty years, he had also served as a director for General Motors. It would be hard to say no to a man I had loved and admired for decades.

"But, Leon," I answered, "what in the world can I say to the most powerful black leaders in the world?" I waited for him to enlighten me.

"Look, Dr. Schuller," Leon dropped the "Bob" and got serious. "You and your wife will fly on the chartered jet with me and my wife. We've leased a 747. The upstairs seats are for those who need privacy and security. There we'll seat Governor Wilder, Dr. Louis Sullivan, Coretta Scott King, Jesse Jackson, and Andy Young. I want Arvella and you to sit next to Mrs. Sullivan and me. *You will go!*"

That settled it! The decision had already been made by the leaders of the conference. I really had no choice. I was highly and humbly honored.

The conference opened in the large ballroom of the InterContinental Hotel. "Remember, Dr. Schuller," I was told, "this is a summit meeting of black leaders. Leaders from the black African nations are here. Also attending are Louis Farrakhan and the widow of Malcolm X. All of them will speak. Just listen, and when you're called to come up and talk, the Lord will tell you what to say."

I listened. Speaker after speaker spoke. Coretta Scott King spoke. Following her was Andrew Young. And, yes, Louis Farrakhan too.

I was struck by the mutual respect shown even among those who shared different faiths and contradictory philosophies.

*Where is the anger?* I thought. I sensed none of it.

Hour after hour I listened. From my seat next to a window, I had a view of the beach. The ocean was calm. From this very spot on the west coast of Africa, cargo boats had been loaded with slaves to be hauled to market. During a period of more than two hundred years, twenty million blacks had been brought from the interior in chains to be sold to the white men who landed their boats on this beach. The entrapped humans had been hauled from this, the eastern border of the Atlantic, to where the waves finally stopped on the eastern shores of the United States.

I was an American citizen because my ancestors had chosen, freely, to immigrate to the United States. But the black Americans in the room were not citizens of the United States by virtue of the free choice of their ancestors. These beautiful, kind, intelligent Americans were the living ancestors of slaves once dragged in chains aboard the ships—right here!

I could see it happening in my mind's eye. Who were those white traders? Were they Dutchmen? Some of them were, yes. I was of Dutch descent. Could one of my ancestors have been involved in slave trading?

I had inherited money from my mother, who had inherited it from her mother, whose father had been—so he claimed—a baron in the Netherlands.

My maternal great grandfather, Gerrit Van Amerongen, had sold all his property in Holland and come to America with his fortune to buy a vast spread in Galveston, Texas, and establish his "empire." A horrendous hurricane later wiped him out, leaving him with only a small portion of his imported wealth.

But from where had my grandfather acquired his wealth? From his father? Could it be that his family in Holland was involved, directly or indirectly, in the slave trade?

These musings released disturbing ideas into my mind as I sat there—a white man from America listening to black speakers, most of them, if not all, descendants of slaves.

For the first time in my life, on the issue of race, I felt the sting of guilt. In my childhood, high school, college, and seminary days, I never felt superior to other races because I was white. I honestly looked on all colors as equals. Being better or worse was a matter of character, not color. But suddenly, here—now—I was drawn back into history when blacks were not equal to whites. They were *better!*

Blacks—morally better than whites? Yes! We whites bought and sold their bodies; they didn't buy and sell us.

Blacks—better patriots than whites? Whites love America, of course! We or ours chose to come to this great country. But blacks love this country with equal passion! How proud they are to be Americans. But neither they nor their ancestors wanted to come here. They were not immigrants—they were imports. They came as products— not people.

Abruptly my thoughts were interrupted as I heard my name called. Loudly! Leon was introducing me as the next speaker. "Let's welcome Dr. Schuller!"

Applause broke out. I found myself almost stumbling through the large crowd. On stage I stepped into Leon's open arms. He beamed, smiled, laughed with pleasure, hugged me, and stepped back—gesturing me to the podium.

I paused. I prayed. I looked into the eyes of the famous black leaders, including Coretta Scott King, Martin Luther King, Jr.'s widow.

What did I think I had to say to them? My prepared speech now seemed absolutely inappropriate.

Suddenly my lips trembled. My face twitched in emotional distress. My heart reached out to these people who loved me. Their grace, affection, and respect reached out to me. I didn't feel that I deserved this. Through my family history I might have been a part of the horrible history of slavery.

I was speechless.

Tears rolled down my cheeks. I prayed silently, "God, let the right words come out." The crowd grew silent, for they could see and sense something strange occurring in the white-haired, white-skinned television preacher they had lovingly invited into their inner circle.

Finally, a few words came. "Thank you for your welcome. I'm so honored to be invited here. But as the only white preacher here, I suddenly, strangely sense for the first time in my life a stab of shame and guilt for what we whites did to blacks."

I couldn't go on. Tears rolled down my face as I heard only a few more words tumble from my trembling lips. "I'm sorry. I'm sorry. I cannot talk. I'm so sorry."

Out of the corner of my eye, I noticed a tall black man standing on stage only a few feet from me. He had come up uninvited. For a brief second our eyes connected. I recognized him as a clergyman of another faith. His eyes sent a message to this speechless preacher: *We don't let someone stand on stage and cry alone.*

I could not deliver a speech. After only a few moments on stage I turned to leave. The audience rose, applauded, and cried. We were one in heart! How strangely my soul, through prayer, had asked for and received forgiveness here in Africa.

## Enjoy the Power of Guilt-Free Living!

Repentance is not shallow, emotional self-condemnation. Real repentance is not pathetic self-flagellation that only deepens personal shame. In such an atmosphere of spiritual pollution, the soul chokes and cannot inhale healthy self-respect. Grinding, blinding, binding guilt prohibits the healthy acceptance and development of a God-intended gift of grace that births "real self-esteem."

Forgiveness must be genuinely extended to the truly repentant. Not to do so is a sin.

But real repentance is an unconditional prerequisite. And does forgiveness always lead to a full restoration of the earlier relationship? Not always. At least not on the human level.

I recall hearing a sermon preached by my minister, Rev. Colenbrander: "God forgives! He will not punish you for sin if you have repented. He will even give you rich and rewarding blessings in the new life you will live in Christ. But the damage done by your sin may remain."

Reverend Colenbrander explained. "When I was a little boy, I did a terrible thing. I hammered a nail into a piece of furniture. My father was so angry, he gave me a spanking. Then he made me extract the nail and promise never again to intentionally damage a beautiful thing.

"I cried. I repented, truly and sincerely. Then my father hugged me, kissed me, and with tears in his eyes said, 'I love you son.'

"Moments passed in the silent embracing. Then, pointing to the damaged table, he said, 'But the hole is still there. It will never go away.' Repentance? Yes! Forgiveness? Yes! But the scars in the memory may remain."

Every person needs to be forgiven sometime by someone for something done or left undone. This generous gift of grace and forgiveness is freely offered by God to any and every person.

Take a chance! Start the adventure! Call for help! He's waiting. He's ready. Get rid of guilt, once and for all. God *forgives!* Enjoy the creative power of guilt-free living!

"As many as received Him, to them He gave the right to become children of God, to those who believe in His name" (John 1:12).

# Chapter 4

# All Things Are Possible...
# Just Ask!

N ow, with the precious gift of the removal of guilt, you can
move on and up in your prayer life with a clean, clear, and
creative connection with God.

ह्ल

**"Help me, Lord! Please, God, lead me to the woman who will
be the right wife for my whole life."**

I prayed this prayer with a passion while I was finishing my
twenty-year educational program to prepare me for my life's work.

I was calling out in a self-centered prayer to the living, loving,
leading Lord I chose to believe and trust. "Help me!"

The God who was slowly but surely answering my first childhood prayer, "Lord, make me a preacher when I grow up," would
give me guidance in life's three basic decisions:

First: What do I want to do and be? That decision was made.

Second: Who and what do I choose to believe? I had made the
irrevocable commitment to believe in the God of Scripture. I would
be a follower of Jesus Christ. He was the world's leading expert on
spiritual truth. He *was* and *is* the Truth!

Now I needed His help with the third basic human decision:
Whom will I marry? Or will I remain single?

The insight I needed began in the hallway outside my psychology class. The instructor, Dr. Lars Grandberg, wisely advised me, "When you get ready to be serious about marriage, start with your head and your heart will follow." To press the point he added strongly, "Never start with your heart. Lead with your head."

God was speaking to me loudly and clearly. I did not fully understand, but my young critical mind accepted that counsel without an ounce of reservation.

"Help, Lord! Tell me the kind of woman I should marry who could help me to become a good preacher," I prayed with a passion.

God answered by providing the criteria: First, she should share my faith. It would also prove helpful if she came from a background in family and religious training as close to mine as possible.

Second, she should enjoy the "ministry," and she should be called and motivated to be a generous and good helpmate to me in my life's work.

Third, she should be attractive to my heart and stimulating to my mind and eye. She should stimulate the desires of both my body and soul.

Fourth, she should be a best friend, someone with whom I could share, talk, visit, and relate. Talking between us should be free, honest, easy, challenging, encouraging, entertaining, enlightening, comforting—and fun.

Now my head was in charge!

At the time I was steadily dating a classmate who was intelligent and attractive. But she came from a culture, family, and community quite unlike my own. My heart felt strongly for her. But suddenly my head did not agree.

Only two weeks later the school year ended. As a seminary student I was assigned a summer job to preach in a vacant Presbyterian church in Preston, Minnesota. I would stop at my home in Iowa on the way to my assignment. No sooner did I reach home than I received a telephone call from an elder at the church in Minnesota.

"Mr. Schuller, you're coming out this week?"

"Yes, sir."

"Well, we're asking you to wait one week. We're not quite ready for you. Okay?"

"No problem," I said, wondering what I would do from this Thursday until the next Thursday.

The telephone rang again. It was a call from a leader in my little country church. "Bob, we remember that wonderful prayer you prayed after the tornado. We were wondering if you could preach this coming Sunday in our church." I was surprised and honored.

"I'd love to," I answered. It would help fill my empty days with study, prayer, and preparation.

Sunday morning arrived. The elder met me at the church and led me to a little room where he introduced me to an attractive, eighteen-year-old organist. She struck me with a stunning, sparkling force I had never before felt.

We discussed the service. She would play the hymns I had chosen. That morning I forgot that I was "going steady." I thanked her for her wonderful work at the keyboard and heard myself say, "What are you doing this week? Would you like to go out with me tomorrow night?"

After a slight pause she accepted my invitation.

We had our first date. She was from my kind of faith, family, community, and church. We talked. We laughed. I believe we held hands as I walked her to the door of her country home—a house as simple as my own.

I drove home, feeling sure she would make a good wife for me.

I went to bed, and when I woke up the next morning, I immediately rushed for pen and paper and wrote a letter to my close friend, Bill Miedema.

"Dear Bill, I've met the girl I'm going to marry. Her name is Arvella DeHaan. She is eighteen years old."

There wasn't a hint of doubt or questioning or indecision in my head—or my heart. I was consumed, not by a person, but by divine destiny.

I've looked back on that moment a thousand or more times. There had to be a God in charge of my life, for truly I could not have "loved her" when I wrote those words. I simply *knew* that I was to marry her. And it would be right.

Four days later I said good-bye and left for my summer job.

æ

The miles separated Arvella and me. I kept in touch throughout the summer. Then Arvella came to Hope College, which was next door to Western Seminary, where I was a student. Our relationship grew and matured. We planned our marriage for the week after I would graduate from seminary.

She would be the person God chose to help make me the preacher I had prayed all my life to become.

Our wedding took place in the middle of the century (1950), in the middle of the year (June), in the middle of the month (the fifteenth).

"Do you take this woman to be your wedded wife?" the officiating minister asked. "If so, answer 'I do.'"

"I do," I answered without hesitation or doubt.

"Will you love her . . ." I heard this phrase like I had never heard it before. "*Will* you *love* her?" It was *future tense.* Not present tense. Without any hesitation or doubt, I answered firmly and optimistically, "I will."

Never would a self-centered prayer be answered by a supreme God more beautifully than my prayer for the right wife. First, a professor's unsolicited advice in a hallway. Next, a church calling me to interrupt my summer work schedule, keeping me home a week. Then, my home church calling to invite me to "preach this Sunday." God answered my prayer! It was a major play in His answering of an earlier prayer, "Lord, make me a preacher when I grow up!"

No one, *no one,* has done more to shape this "preacher" more wisely and wonderfully than Arvella. I have listened and learned from her and am always lifted by her.

As this book is written, Arvella and I are planning our forty-fifth wedding anniversary. Our five children and seventeen grandchildren are planning to be with us.

# God Always Answers Positive Prayers

God hears. God cares. God answers.

"But when?" our soul cries out.

"Wait," is the only answer we can find in the Bible. "Wait on the LORD; / Be of good courage, / And He shall strengthen your heart" (Ps. 27:14). "Call to Me, and I will answer you, and show you great and mighty things, which you do not know" (Jer. 33:3).

As I wrote these words, I heard the telephone ring. I picked up the receiver just as the caller hung up. Someone was so close to connecting. If he or she had only waited seconds more.

When you call for help, know that God will answer. Don't hang up until you give Him time to make the connection! In my soul's journey, I've learned that God always answers positive prayers. I once summed up, in a sermon, how He does it:

**When the call for help is not right,**
  **God answers, "No."**
**Trust Him. He'll come up with a better idea or better timing or better people.**

**When the call for help is ill-timed,**
  **God answers, "Slow."**
**Wait! Till He brings the right person, project, purpose, and plan together.**

**When the call for help finds you ill-prepared or ill-equipped to receive the blessing,**
  **God answers, "Grow."**
**He'll shape and sculpt you, connect and correct you.**

**When everyone and everything is in place,**
  **God answers, "Go." Now! Share your dream!**
**And mountains move. Miracles happen. Your prayer is answered.**

Yes, prayer on Level Two is prayer of the self-centered kind. And that's not only okay—it's terribly important.

Jesus prayed on this level too. In Mark 14:36 we hear him crying out for help:

"Father, all things are possible for You." (A Level One prayer.) "Take this cup away from Me." (A Level Two prayer.)

We had better pray for ourselves. We have important needs: We need light. We need help. We need guidance. We need encouragement, insight, correction, and paradigm shifts. God only knows how much poverty and pain we endure because we do not call for help. "You do not have because you do not ask. You ask and do not receive, because you ask amiss" (James 4:2–3).

My witness is that God gives us dreams that are bigger than we are. Achieving these dreams is impossible if we try to achieve them all alone or only with people we like, agree with, are related to, or who share our religion.

God may know that the key person is someone you don't know or someone who at this moment is a competitor or someone with whom you are in conflict.

Call to Him: "Lord, I don't want your dream to fail. I'm not ego driven. I'm driven by *Your* dream. I must not fail. I don't want my own way—I only want to succeed as your servant."

*We need help!* God's help!

## All Possibilities Exhausted?

I was twenty-eight years old when I arrived in California to start a church. My wife was my only member. We had exhausted all possibilities when, desperate to find a place to start preaching, I went to a drive-in theater.

I learned a powerful lesson God was teaching me. Simply put: "When you've exhausted all possibilities, remember this: *You haven't.*"

The owner of the drive-in raised his eyebrows and laughed. "You want to do *what?* Start a church on Sunday mornings in my drive-in theater?"

He was a Christian. A Lutheran. He shook his head in disbelief as he answered, "Well, I don't mind. Okay. You can use it. But I'll have to charge you ten dollars for the sound man to come out and turn the power on."

That open-air church would be my Sunday home for more than five years. God wanted to shape me, change me, prepare me. He did.

I fell in love again with the sky. With the white clouds I loved as a child by the river in Iowa. With the sun. With the tips of eucalyptus trees bending slowly in the breeze. With the birds on free and happy wing. I was back in the beauty of God's creation.

Week after week. Month after month. Year after year. Slowly my congregation grew from two members, Arvella and I, to two hundred new friends. We eventually collected a few dollars. The first offering was $83.75 from strangers who trusted me before I had a chance to prove myself. We saved our money carefully, secured a bank loan, and built a small chapel seating 150 persons.

໖

No matter how many dreams we dream, no matter how many mountains we see moved, no matter how many miles we walk in our soul's adventure with God, we never get too big, too strong, too smart, or too old to pray this simple prayer: "I need help. I can't do it alone. Help me, Lord."

Sometimes we need help for a mess we've made, for success we must manage, and for the stress that is never far from us.

Sometimes we need help when people have messed with us. Yes, I, too, have been victimized.

# On Trial

Unfair attacks have come from atheists, from evil persons who correctly see my ministry as a threat to their sinful businesses, and, sadly, from well-meaning, sincere, Bible-believing, born-again Christians.

I remember Billy Graham saying once, "The worst criticism against me has not come from people of other faiths but from other Christians." Ditto, Billy!

Yes, I've been falsely accused. Here's one: "He's not accountable theologically or financially."

A gross lie. Most of my accusers are not accountable. Journalists—including TV anchors—are not accountable to anyone except the readers of the rating charts. If they can sell newspapers, books, or TV air time, they're *in!* If not—however good they may be—they're *out*. They are controlled by the market not the Master.

The widespread expansion of "independent" churches that are "nondenominational" does give me concern. Here the pastors are not accountable to anyone except their church board. In many cases the pastor can control by political manipulation the makeup of the board to ensure a majority who will back him. And the minority vote has no course of higher appeal, no one to hear their critical voices, which may be right on.

Billy Graham saw this danger and launched a worldwide theological endorsement arrangement for evangelists—many of whom had no group to whom they were accountable. Hence was born "The Lausanne Covenant."

Thank you, Billy. I signed it, even though I am involved in a much older denominational accountability arrangement. Dr. Graham also led the move to establish an evangelical financial accountability organization.

I have always been and remain accountable to the *Book of Church Order* of the Reformed Church in America.

"You should leave the denomination and be independent," I was advised years ago. I would save money. Our church, which has thousands of members, pays the denomination an assessed fee based on membership. It would be "cheaper" to simply join the new evangelical financial accountability group.

But I respect the *Book of Church Order,* written and revised over a few hundred years. At any time my phone could ring. The denominational officer could request to meet with me to "ask some questions." I would have to concur—or get out.

Such accountability places sensible, subconscious, and serious restraint on my lifestyle, my preaching and teaching, and my moral and financial behavior.

For me, total freedom and complete independence could breed arrogance and potential danger.

If I do or teach something that is wrong, my board of directors could ask me to give an account. If I am upheld by a simple majority, I'm okay. But the minority would have the right to appeal the case against me to a higher court. In our denomination that is called "The Classis."

I had that experience. I was falsely accused by a minority in the church led by an assistant minister whom I did not choose and who did not come from my denominational college, seminary, and tradition. He led a few good people to conspire against me. The issue came to a head at our board meeting.

Dr. Wilfred Landrus—a charter member, an elder, a professor of educational psychology at Chapman College, and a devout Christian—brought the silent issue into the open.

"There is a rumor going around that our pastor, Reverend Schuller, is guilty of false teachings and bad leadership," he said. "I suggest that we pass a resolution affirming, encouraging, and supporting him. If you have doubts, vote no. If you agree with the resolution, vote yes."

Dr. Landrus then made the motion: "I so move." He added one sentence. "All in favor will vote 'yes' by standing. All who oppose will vote 'no' by remaining seated."

There were seventeen people present at that meeting. I could hear folding chairs squeak as people began to stand. I lifted my head and, through tears, saw the smiles of fifteen standing members. Two people had remained seated.

I was free to dream God's dream again! I was most certainly on the receiving end of the prayers of the people of God. They were praying for me with faith.

But I was in for something few ministers in my denomination have ever faced in its more than three centuries of existence.

The two dissident elders were advised of their rights. They could appeal the decision to the higher court. They did.

"Help me, Lord!" I prayed.

The Classis received their formal request, and the stated clerk—the top official—agreed to hear the case. Appropriately, he appointed a special jury made up of himself as chairman and three other ministers.

The case was heard on a Wednesday night. The two accusers were there. So was I. The plaintiffs handed a letter to the stated clerk, who excused the defendant and the plaintiffs.

We were called back in thirty minutes. The stated clerk spoke. "In our professional opinion, there is no evidence of any moral, financial, or theological errors by Reverend Schuller."

They explained to the two dissenting elders, who had come into our church from different denominational backgrounds, that "The Reformed Church in America requires its ministers to sign an agreement to live by the historic Christian creeds: the Apostles' Creed, the Athanasian Creed, the Nicene Creed, and the Heidelberg Catechism.

"Reverend Schuller has signed to accept these confessional standards as guidance in his interpretations of holy Scriptures. There is no evidence that he has in written or spoken word rejected these teachings. He may have questions—even doubts—about some of the details contained therein. He has that liberty, so long as he can live quietly with them and does not in his public professional work take issue by voicing his reservations on a public platform." They continued, "We see the thirty-two charges against him as merely conflict in personality, and we recommend the case be dismissed without further consideration."

I was grateful, but I insisted, "Sirs, please have all thirty-two charges read aloud to me. Give me the opportunity to address each charge." They agreed.

Some charges were ecclesiastical—arguments that had divided Protestants into more than three hundred denominations and sects in the United States. They did not deserve to be dealt with.

Some were serious: "Dr. Schuller doesn't preach against Satan or hell."

I answered that one. "Satan? I don't know him personally as well as I know Jesus Christ. I choose to honor Jesus Christ. He knows better than I the truth about Satan. I don't deny that Satan exists. I just focus on the Lord, who alone inspires us, saves us, and preserves our souls."

The denomination leaders smiled and nodded their heads in agreement.

"Hell?" I said, "I know very little about it. I only know I'm not going there. And I don't want to frighten people into becoming Christians. I choose to believe that people should be motivated to become Christians not out of a fear of hell or in search of a reward in heaven. I want people to become Christians out of a desire to become beautiful persons who will live and love and lift the levels of other lives around them by becoming like Jesus Christ, by having minds through which Christ can think, faces through which Christ can glow, hearts through which Christ can love, tongues through which Christ can speak words of hope."

The trial was over. All charges were dismissed. The jury was unanimous in their decision. My honor was vindicated and restored.

The presiding officer at the trial had been my "boss," Rev. Gradus Vander Linden. When I was criticized for preaching in a drive-in theater, he came to my defense. He was my bishop until his death. He believed in me. He prayed for me. I still miss him. He was a truly great leader in our denomination.

Now I was driven with a passion to purge from Christianity the negative spirit that could embarrass, humiliate, shame, dishonor, demean, or disgrace another human being.

I had been spared and saved by the God who was still remembering my first childhood prayer. I thank God for the prayers of His people, which sustained me.

I thank God for my denomination, which lives with such a wise and wonderful *Book of Church Order.*

I thank God for carrying my soul successfully through this dramatic adventure.

I know the truth of the apostle Paul's words: "Confident of this very thing, that He who has begun a good work in you will complete it" (Phil. 1:6).

Victimized? Well, maybe. But you will understand why I was so moved to receive the following letter in the fortieth anniversary year of our church's ministry:

**The Reformed Church in America**
**Policy, Planning, and Administration Services**
**David W. Schreuder, Acting Director/Secretary**
**for General Synod Operations**
**William T. Burns, Associate**
**for General Synod Operations**

**June 28, 1994**

**The Rev. Dr. Robert H. and Arvella Schuller**
**The Crystal Cathedral**
**12141 Lewis Street**
**Garden Grove, CA 92640**

**Dear Dr. and Mrs. Schuller:**

**It gives me great pleasure to inform you that the General Synod Supreme Court of The Reformed Church in America in its 188th annual session convened on the campus of Central College in Pella, Iowa, from June 6–10, 1994 resolved:**

**WHEREAS in September 1955 The Reformed Church in America began a new church in Garden Grove, California, and**

called the Rev. Robert H. Schuller to be the founding pastor,
and almost forty years later the ministry of the Crystal
Cathedral has positively influenced the lives of people around
the world for the glory of God; and

WHEREAS through the outreach of *The Hour of Power,* the
positive preaching of the Rev. Robert H. Schuller, the Crystal
Cathedral educational ministry, and through the commitment
of thousands of Crystal Cathedral members, people from all
walks of life and pastors of Christ's church have discovered
the hope of Jesus Christ and the inspiration of the Holy Spirit;

THEREFORE BE IT RESOLVED that the one hundred
eighty-eighth session of the General Synod of The Reformed
Church in America, meeting in Pella, Iowa, on the tenth day of
June 1994 extends to the Rev. Robert and Arvella Schuller its
most sincere congratulations in this fortieth year of ministry
of the Crystal Cathedral; and

BE IT FURTHER RESOLVED to give their thanks to God for the
Rev. Robert and Arvella Schuller and their ceaseless
commitment to the Lord, their faithful dedication to The
Reformed Church in America, and their unending challenge to
help individuals discover God's image within them and to
encourage individuals to recognize possibilities for new life in
Christ, and pray for God's continuing blessing for the ministry
of the Crystal Cathedral into the twenty-first century and
beyond.

There will never be adequate words to express the significance
of your ministry over the past four decades.

On a personal note, I too am thankful for your ministry and
for the opportunity you gave to me to serve as pastor to single

adults at the Crystal Cathedral, 1984–87. I treasure the
memories and experiences of those years.

May God's richest blessings continue in abundance for your
ministry in the years ahead.

Sincerely,
David W. Schreuder

# Make Your Prayers Big Enough

Twenty years later. With ten thousand members, we now had the
largest Reformed Church in the world, and we needed a larger church
building to house the people.

"Help me, Lord!" I prayed.

I found myself longing for the sky, the sun, the moon at night,
the sight of tender tips of trees bowing reverently to the invisible
breeze.

"Can't you make it all glass?" I heard myself say to the architect,
Philip Johnson. The divine dream had surpassed human reality.

"A building to seat three thousand people and *all glass?* In an
earthquake zone? That's impossible. But we'll try," he answered.

Six weeks later he called to show me his plans. My heart sank: an
all-glass roof—but solid walls. "We need the solid walls for engineering
stability," he explained. I didn't understand, and I wasn't impressed.
He read my polite dissatisfaction. "Hire smarter engineers," I challenged. "I want it all glass. I want to see the *whole tree,*" I argued.
"From the strong trunk to the tender tip."

He threw up his hands, rolled up the plans, and left.

Another six weeks passed. Another call. Another meeting. Philip
came in carrying an aluminum case. He opened it, and I was blown
away. Inside was a star-shaped, all-glass model of a great cathedral.

"The Crystal Cathedral!" I blurted out. "But it's a mirror from
the outside. You can't see in."

"We have to deflect the sun to keep the temperature comfortable," he said. "But from the inside it's one big window to look out. And as you said, Dr. Schuller, you will see the white clouds sliding silently through the silent sea of space."

"It's fantastic! We'll build it!" I declared, making the decision before I had solved the mountainous problems its construction would entail.

A passionate dream generated by Possibility Thinking consumed me. I was into prayer—Level One!

"How much will it cost?" I asked.

"Seven million dollars," he answered.

This was a challenge that far surpassed our known resources. We needed enormous help. I shifted prayer gears up to Level Two.

I was overwhelmed by a new and rough reality. This was 1976. The next year, 1977, inflation soared to 30 percent. It would soar in 1978 to 33 percent. Likewise in 1979. Interest rates would rise from 9 percent to 22 percent.

Never before—maybe never again—was a commitment made to an impossible dream in such impossible economic times!

"Make your prayers big enough for God to fit in." This amazing sentence grabbed hold of me. It was what the mind of this preacher named Schuller needed to hear.

Two years before, we had hired an architect who designed a large but basic building he said would cost four million. We had a professional fund-raising campaign with a slogan—"Impact."

We didn't even make a dent. The people simply were not motivated to give. We failed.

Now we were going to try again with a new architect and a new plan—almost double the cost!

I prayed. This was big enough to let God take over! He did. He gave me a bigger, better idea: *Don't start unless and until you get a leadoff gift of one million dollars in cash.*

I prayed deeper and bigger prayers.

Think big! Think bigger! *It costs no more to pray a big prayer than it does to pray a small prayer,* I thought.

At that very time, I "accidentally" (no, providentially!) read a story in the newspaper about a man representing one family who had given a million dollars for the construction of a new YMCA building in Anaheim. I had never heard of him before.

I found his address and arranged to visit him. I showed him and his wife the Crystal Cathedral plans. They were impressed.

"How much will it cost?" he asked.

"Seven million," I answered.

"How much do you have?" he asked.

"Nothing," I answered, "and everybody knows that. No one will believe in me or my dream unless we have a cash leadoff gift of one million dollars."

Silence.

"Would you like to give that gift?" I asked.

His answer was instant and firm. "I'd like to, but I can't."

My next move shocked even me. It was impetuous. I didn't think before I spoke.

"Then may I pray before I leave?"

"Sure. Go ahead."

These words tumbled out of my mouth:

**"Dear God, I'm so thankful that he said he'd like to give. Was it Your idea or was it mine to ask John Crean to give a million dollars? If it was my idea, forgive me, and help him to forgive me too. But if it was Your idea, can You figure out a way for him to do what he'd like to—but can't? Amen."**

He stood up. We shook hands and walked to the car. Politely we said good-bye.

The next morning at 11:05 A.M. my office phone rang.

"Schuller? It's Crean. I don't know when, and I don't know how, but I will!"

Never before and never since have I experienced the presence of a real, living God like I felt His presence in that holy moment.

I shouted! I wept.

Sixty days later, the Creans gave us shares in their company that cashed out for one million dollars!

ઢ

It would be tragic for me, if when I stand before God, He tells me all of the things I could have done for Him and the human family if I had only been humble enough and brave enough to ask for *help!*

# I REALLY CARE ABOUT YOU!

*Unselfish love: Here's where my prayer to a living, loving God grows to a higher level and glows with a holier light.*

"'YOU SHALL LOVE THE LORD YOUR GOD WITH ALL YOUR HEART,
WITH ALL YOUR SOUL, AND WITH ALL YOUR MIND.' THIS IS THE
FIRST AND GREAT COMMANDMENT. AND THE SECOND IS LIKE IT:
'YOU SHALL LOVE YOUR NEIGHBOR AS YOURSELF.'"

— MATTHEW 22:37–39 —

# Chapter 5

# I'll Pray for You

You are ready for Level Three of the prayer adventure—you will forget about yourself. Now you are caught up in selfless concern and care for others. "Please!" you say to God, with reverence, urgency, passion, and confidence. "Please, Lord, touch the one who is in need or pain."

I've prayed for others tens of thousands of times and have seen miracles happen.

But I will tell you about the times, too, when my prayers were not answered as I passionately prayed they would be. Husbands, wives, sons, and daughters died. Divorces were filed. Bankruptcies were finalized. Limbs were amputated.

"Why?"

That's one question God never answers. Even His Son on a cross asked Him "Why?" And God never spoke a word.

It's understandable why God remains silent. People who ask "why" don't want an answer. They want an argument. God walks away from arguments. He won't be drawn in.

Hurting hearts don't want explanations. They would only challenge the answer with another question. "But *why* that way? *Why* now? *Why* me?"

True, permanent healing will happen only when God takes us into eternity, where there will be total, complete, perfect understanding and a pure perception of the whole complex picture.

Somehow, we must say what saints have said for centuries: "Not my will—but Yours be done."

# Only Broken Hearts Will Do

Prayer on this intercessory level is high on the "unselfish" scale. "I'll pray for you" is one of the most encouraging, affirming promises we can make to our suffering families and friends.

Level Two prayers for "Help!" may not be answered unless we move on to Level Three, where we forget our appropriate but self-centered prayers and are refocused on "ministry"—reaching people who need hope and help.

It hurt me more to see my only son lose his first wife than it did to see my teenage daughter lose her leg or to see Arvella lose a breast.

My wife and I were raised in families in which there had never in history been a marriage broken by a divorce—until Uncle Henry's only son went through it. Even then we tried to ignore it. We rationalized that he was paying a price for his career as a professional marine officer.

Then divorce happened to *our* family. I had to come to grips with the limitation of Possibility Thinking. It didn't seem to control other people over whom we had no control.

The divine dilemma all over again. God created people—not computers. People have the freedom to say "no." Without that choice, "yes" would have no meaning, no morality, and surely no value.

I don't remember how we got the word. All I can remember is crying, weeping, hurting. For my daughter-in-law. For my son. For the children who would be torn apart in the divorce.

I remember meeting my son in a private place. He had been well trained in the best undergraduate and graduate schools for his life's calling—the ministry. "But you won't have to leave the ministry," I tried to tell him. "You are ordained by God, and God is not divorcing you."

I cried as I hugged him. The emotional words were words of grief. It was the hardest moment in my whole life.

"I'll have to tell my congregation tomorrow in Sunday morning worship," he said, looking at me with a hurt and horror I had not seen in his eyes before.

I had often prayed that God would bless his ministry, "even though his heart had never been broken." I had, after all, frequently quoted the classic line, "In love's service, only broken hearts will do."

Well, now his heart was broken.

We cried. We prayed.

The next morning, robed in the gown of an ordained clergyman, he walked into his pulpit and told his loving congregation that he had an important announcement to make.

It was short, and when he turned his humiliated back to the flock, they could see his broad shoulders heave. Even with his microphone turned off they could hear the mournful sobbing. It broke the stunned silence.

Quietly someone from the congregation rose, walked to the altar, and put his hands on Robert's trembling back. Someone else followed, and then another. Then many men and women—young, middle-aged, and old—engulfed him in their tears and their prayers.

I cannot count the prayers prayed for him in the months that followed.

I know that the divorce was not God's will. I know God's will was a successful ministry He planned to give that young man. God never quits. God never lets bad news remain the last news.

Today that brokenhearted minister is a stronger, wiser, more compassionate, more tenderhearted and caring person because of the painful divorce he endured. He can minister to people who have been hurt as he has been hurt.

Later, that same church was filled to overflowing when Robert tearfully stood at the altar to marry his second wife, Donna. He had invited the entire congregation: "You wept with me in my grief; now rejoice with me in my joy."

So the tears flowed again, tears of tremendous love from his people and tears of joy. Standing beside Robert were the two children from his first marriage. Two more precious children have since been born. They are all beautiful children. Prayers for them are being answered by a God who never stops blessing people who pray from step to step, from stage to stage.

# Believe What You Preach!

Please! Intercession. Prayer on the Third Level. There is a God who is listening, who's never out of touch, who's consistently as close to us as thoughts in our brains and feelings in our hearts. He lives! He loves! He listens! He connects when we reach out!

As a young pastor I needed to really believe God answers prayer. I could not and would not preach something out of my head that didn't start in my heart.

I still prepare my messages that way. I start with my heart so that I will always be sincere. There is no compensation for the absence of sincerity.

In my soul's adventure with God in prayer, I witnessed with my own eyes a remarkable illustration of the fact that real prayer really works.

Before the Crystal Cathedral was built, we were meeting in a large facility that today serves as a beautiful dining hall. It was our worship center. The pulpit stood high, with a view of the parking lot through a wall of glass that ran from the rear to the front of the church. Alongside this wall of glass was a 200-foot-long, 12-foot-wide pool of water.

Beneath the pulpit and the choir loft there was a large choir rehearsal room.

On Sunday mornings I would usually stop to greet the choir, pray with them, and then lead them into church where the service would begin.

One Sunday I impulsively, without conscious thought or planning, said something that shocked me as I heard my mouth say it. I was prepared to speak that morning on prayer. I needed and wanted a fresh, honest story to tell that would support and illustrate my teaching on "Real Prayer Really Works."

"Good morning," I greeted the choir enthusiastically. "Let's have prayer." Then a very unusual prayer spilled out: "Lord, we are here to think about You. Right now, reach out to find someone who is out there with no intention of going to church. Interrupt his life, and motivate him to do what he would never do—suddenly decide to come to church. Here, let me speak to him. Let the choir sing to him. Amen."

Prayer on Level Three—we were praying for someone we did not even know!

What happened next was one of the most dramatic answers to prayer I've ever experienced. We left the choir room and proceeded down the long center aisle. I walked into the pulpit with the choir behind me.

About five minutes into my sermon, it happened.

I looked through the glass wall. It was a sunny and warm California morning. But coming off the street and walking across the parking lot was a tall man wearing a long brown double-breasted overcoat—buttoned and belted! He looked totally out of place. Never before had I seen anyone come to a California church service dressed like this.

And he kept coming, walking to the spot in the glass wall directly in front of me. Then he walked along the pool to the front entrance. After entering the church he walked up the center aisle slowly, studying the crowd, looking and acting terribly out of place. The choir gaped. I struggled to keep focused on the words of my sermon. To the very first pew he came, sat down, folded his hands across his lap, looked up, and listened to the entire sermon. And he never removed his overcoat! I rushed to the rear of the sanctuary at the end of the service so I could reach out to him.

"You're visiting today?" was my conversation opener.

"Yes, sir," he answered politely. "I am an itinerant, sir, and I slept under the bridge over there." He pointed in the direction where a railroad bridge went over a dry river bed. "And as I started out this morning, I saw this cross. *What's that?* I wondered. I never go to church, but I couldn't resist this strong impulse that came over me to check this out and see what it was all about."

Before I could respond, he smiled and said, "I liked it. Thank you. I've got to be on my way."

I'm sure some of the choir members may have been tempted to believe the whole scene was a Schuller setup! Never did I preach with more conviction and passion than I did that morning on the topic "Real Prayer Really Works."

Prayer—my soul's adventure with God. He gave that one to me! My request was granted. My will was His will too. I'm sure He prompted that unthinkable prayer from my lips to the choir and had the answer all set up so we wouldn't miss the miracle. He wanted to teach a young preacher to really, truly believe what he was prepared to preach.

"Lord, make me a preacher when I grow up!" He was still answering that prayer.

## How Can I Pray for Those I Cannot Love?

What about enemies? It's easy to pray for others if I love them. But can I pray for someone I have a hard time liking?

In my whole life, no lesson on prayer helped me more than something I learned from one of the great saints of this century, Frank Laubach. He preached in our church. He was a world figure of immense spiritual stature. He founded the greatest literacy movement of the twentieth century. I loved him.

"Love is what we need," he preached. "We must love and pray for our enemies too!"

"But how can I pray for those I cannot love?" I asked him. "The Russian communists are threatening a third world war!"

"Pray for them," he said. "God can hear and answer that prayer too!"

I did. (Was that the seed of prayer that a quarter of a century later would enable me to become the first minister to preach about Jesus Christ to the entire Soviet empire over their atheist television network?)

"But, Dr. Laubach, there are people I know who are selfish, greedy, *mean!* I cannot love a person like that. Maybe I am supposed to, but I have to tell you, I'd be a hypocrite if I said, 'I love that person.'"

"Bob, you are right. You are not Jesus. He can love someone even if you cannot. The answer to your predicament is prayer.

"You just must not get in Jesus Christ's way," he continued. "Let *Him* love that person. Don't block Christ's love from reaching out to him or her."

He went on, giving me a lesson that I would never forget.

"Pray this way, Bob. When you see someone you have trouble loving or praying for, take your left hand (mentally, if not physically), open your palm, and reach straight up to the sky. Now take your right hand, point your index finger straight out like it is an arrow in the bow. Point to that problem person. Now pray, 'Lord, I'm supposed to love him. I don't love him. I am not able to love him. But You can. And I won't obstruct You. Fall into my upraised palm, Holy Spirit, flow down through my arm, through my heart and my chest, into my right arm, down to my pointing finger, and strike him with *Your love.*'"

The next day an obnoxious, irreverent, profane salesman came— unwelcome and uninvited—to call on me. "Oh no! Not him!" I mumbled as I saw him get out of his car. Then I remembered what Dr. Laubach had told me. I retreated to a corner of my room, assumed the "Laubach Prayer Position," and let Christ "shoot out His invisible love."

A miracle happened! When the salesman stepped into my study, he was different! He was not repulsive. He was warm and friendly; he radiated kindness and gentleness! I actually liked the guy.

He never knew what hit him!

# Do I Have to Pray for My Enemies?

I've had my share of enemies.

Building the Crystal Cathedral brought them out in force. Some were Christians. "Schuller should have spent that money on foreign missions."

Some were atheists. "He is spending millions on another monument to superstition."

Some were religious but not Christians. "He should have given the money to feed the poor."

I prayed for all of them when they attacked.

"How could you possibly sink millions into that monument to your ego?" I was asked on a live radio show in an eastern city.

"To begin with," I answered, "I believe God dreamed it. He entrusted His dream with me. It was His idea before it was given to me.

"I prayed constantly for God's guidance. Then I prayed that He would bring solutions to problems, including money. Five gifts of one million dollars each were brought to us by God's friends, whom He inspired to help build His dream.

"But I have to tell you," I went on, "I have watched that building get built. Not one dollar is left in that cathedral! No dollar bills, no coins are in the cement, glass, or steel. The money didn't go into the cathedral. It all went into checks made out to laborers. Some from faraway states where iron was mined. Where glass was made. Where gas was bought for trucks to haul the product to our property.

"All the money went to workers. They spent it on food, house payments, gifts to charities, and children's college savings funds."

So God answered my prayers on the intercessory level as I prayed for my critics. It kept me healthy. And happy too.

Then there was the adventure of my soul with my God as we journeyed together through the late 1980s "television evangelist scandals."

I did not know Jimmy Swaggart. We met face-to-face once, briefly, and we verbalized greetings. I do not recall handshakes. He was attacking me—along with Mother Teresa—by name, on his television shows at the time.

I did know Jim and Tammy Bakker. Like Jimmy Swaggart, the Bakkers did not come up through an old mainline Protestant denomination but through a twentieth-century movement that did not require pastors to have an undergraduate and graduate education. The scandals were shocking. But the media didn't take notice of the differences that existed in denominational training of evangelists and ministers.

My name would be linked without distinction to all the others. I would go through very hard times.

Kenneth Woodward, religious writer for *Newsweek,* would appear on *Nightline* with Ted Koppel and challenge the media to investigate "all of them." He dropped my name too.

*The Los Angeles Times* and the *Orange County Register* could not ignore the challenge to investigate me. Every private and public area of my life was probed and examined. People were offered cash with guarantees of anonymity if they could "come up with something on Schuller." I found out that it is not illegal for an investigative reporter to pay off "donors of information" and not be obligated to disclose their names.

Accountability? Where was it in the profession of journalism?

After six months of painful, humiliating exposure to suspicious investigative reporters, *The Los Angles Times* broke the story—a full page—with this big, bold headline: "Crystal Cathedral Unscathed."

# Pray and God Will Find a Way

How beautifully God answers prayer. How? Often in ways and through persons, processes, and events that leave us speechless.

"Dr. Schuller, you have to come with me." It was Congressman Clyde Doyle on the telephone. "I want to take you fishing on the Pacific Ocean. I am taking my only sister. She has been through such tragedy."

She had gone through great grief. Her son died at the age of eighteen in surgery. And her remaining child, a daughter, died a year later in an auto accident at the age of seventeen. And now her husband was also gone.

"How did you survive?" I asked her.

"By prayer, Reverend Schuller. I live in Long Beach, near the ocean. Every day I would walk to the beach to sit alone and watch the waves come and go.

"Day after day, month after month, year after year. Until one day, like every other day, as I sat and talked to God, it happened.

"A wave came and swished in front of me. It was like a smile from the secret, silent depths of creation. Then the wave slipped back to the eternal deep from where it had come. Then this strong, powerful sentence came into my consciousness. 'There is nothing but life! And it is eternal.'

"All of the pain in my hollowed-out heart was swept away with that wave. My memory, which was one deep black hole, was suddenly flooded with a divine light! God was filling me with peace. He spoke through a speechless wave!"

Another prayer surprise: Hazel Wright was a philanthropist who had lived in Chicago. Now she lived in Palm Springs, where her generous financial gift had deservedly put her name on a beautiful wing of the Eisenhower Medical Center.

I was told she was dying. I loved her dearly; she was a precious friend. Now cancer was about to bring her to the moment when she would make her transition into eternity.

Outside her room I was briefed. "She may have only an hour or two to live. She is in a death coma. She cannot communicate. She doesn't know that she is dying. But thank you for coming, Dr. Schuller. You have been her pastor for years. Maybe you can just say a silent prayer over her."

I walked in and was left alone with her, as I had requested.

She had given so much love—and lift—to my ministry. I silently prayed that God would put strong wings on her soul, which was about to slip away to her heavenly home.

Then I spoke, quietly.

"Hazel. It's Bob Schuller, your pastor. Can you hear me?" No response. I touched her forehead. "I'm here, Hazel." I watched for some reaction. There was no sign of life, only her quiet breathing.

Then a strange spirit moved through me, strange because I had never before stood by the bedside of a dying friend feeling the strong impulse to "give a dying soul a farewell gift." She had given so much to me and mine, including the largest church pipe organ in America, which was now housed in the four inner points of the star-shaped Crystal Cathedral. Even critics say it is the most exciting pipe organ in the world. The organ had been her gift to the millions of music lovers who viewed *The Hour of Power.*

Now, dying on a hospital bed, she couldn't see. Or hear. What could I give her?

I prayed. Suddenly I saw it—a long-stemmed rose in a vase at her bedside. An amazing, beautiful idea struck me: *Take the rose out of its vase and place the fresh opening bud above her lips.* I did. The velvety red petals touched her nostrils. *Could she possibly breathe in the fragrance?* I wondered.

Suddenly, softly, sweetly, she smiled!

Hazel had received her gift! Her last remaining faculty was the gift of smell. Only God knew that, and He had guided me! He hears us when we say "Please!" on behalf of others.

# The Day Tears "Talked"

I was taught in seminary, "never assume that a person who is in a death coma is incapable of hearing. They probably just can't respond."

The call came that Stanley Reimer, a beloved friend and a beautiful elder on our church board, was on his way to the hospital with a heart attack. "He'll probably be dead on arrival at the emergency room," I was told.

A fast drive to the hospital. "He's still alive," I was told when I arrived. "In intensive care."

As I stepped in, his doctor drew back from the bed, dropped his head, and said, "He's alive—but he's dying, Reverend Schuller. He's gone for all practical purposes."

I was shocked that the doctor spoke the words *out loud,* within a few feet of Stanley's ears! What if Stanley could still hear but could not respond with speech or touch? I thought this was terribly unprofessional behavior. Without another word the doctor left.

"Stanley," I spoke softly, but strongly, my lips only inches from his ear. "Stanley, it's Dr. Schuller. I've come to ask our God to save your life! Stanley, I telephoned the church. Countless prayers are being sent to God right now for you. Stanley, you had a twenty-minute cardiac arrest. You're hurt—badly. But you will recover, Stanley!"

Tears filled his eyes and rolled down his cheeks. He heard me! "I hear you, Stanley! Your tears are speaking when your lips cannot. You heard me!" More tears came—his and mine.

In a matter of hours, Stanley's eyes opened. Speech—slurred but understandable—returned! He recovered, not completely, but enough to live, laugh, talk, and pray joyful prayers for another ten years. And he *never* forgot that day when the miracle of new life was given by God in answer to prayer.

Prayers for others. Intercession. Level Three. Here's where your faith in a living, loving God grows and glows.

## Prayer Saves an Innocent Life

Pray! Even when the answer is half a world away. Yes, pray even if the answer lies in the hands of those who may not share the faith.

The Bible says that it is "good and acceptable" to pray for the leaders of our government—for "all who are in authority" (1 Tim. 2:2–3).

I was scheduled to be in Washington, D.C., for a speaking engagement. I arranged for a private appointment with President George Bush in the Oval Office. Only one day before my appointment, the headline news broke: "American hostage hanged by Arab terrorists in Lebanon." Then the warning: "The second execution will happen in twenty-four hours unless the president of the United States releases the Arab prisoners held in Israel."

I called the president's office. "My appointment is tomorrow morning at 11:00 A.M. The twenty-four hours the terrorists gave President Bush are up at 3:00 P.M. Shall we reschedule the appointment?"

The answer came back later that afternoon: "The president is going to be up late tonight calling leaders all over the world. He is putting everything else aside. But he wants to keep his appointment with you, Dr. Schuller, if at all possible. So come in as planned at 11:00 tomorrow morning."

I had been with President Bush in the Oval Office before, but that morning his face showed unhidden and undisguised grief, anguish, even fear. "I don't know what I can do at this late hour. I've talked to Arab and Palestinian and Muslim leaders all over the world. None of them can or will be helpful. The only answer I get is 'Let the prisoners go! And save an American from certain death. We can't stop them. Only you can do that.' But, Bob, we cannot, we must not, yield to ransom demands."

The president was in profound pain and distress. He went on, "There's only one other person whose advice I've not gotten. He's in Oman. I can't reach him."

President Bush looked at me with a dejected, frustrated stare. It was now close to noon. Only three hours were left.

"May I pray?" I asked.

"Oh yes, please. Please do," he answered.

We stood in the middle of the room. Just then, before I could utter a word of prayer, the president's secretary walked in and handed him a note. As he read it his face lifted, "Bob, it's the man from Oman. He's on the line! I'll have to pick up the phone." He moved toward the phone on his desk. He stopped and turned around. "Let's pray first. He'll wait," he said.

I put my hands on his shoulders. My eyes were open. His were squeezed tightly shut. His head and shoulders drooped. My prayer was short and swift: "Thank You, God, for the man on the telephone. Use him, good Father, to talk the terrorists out of their planned execution. Thank You, God, that he's on the line now. Thank You that they found him. Thank You, God, that he's willing to talk to the president. Put the right words on the president's lips. Save the innocent American's life without rewarding the kidnappers by releasing their friends. Amen."

The president gripped my hand and forearm; his eyes were misty. "Thank you, Bob," he said as he moved swiftly to his desk, waving good-bye to me while I excused myself.

Four hours later it was a lead story on CNN. Good news was reported: "The hostage was released with no ransom paid." Then the news anchor added, "No reason for this change of heart was given. Perhaps it was the prayer President Bush had with Reverend Robert Schuller, with whom he prayed in the Oval Office only three hours before the execution was to occur."

Our loving Father in heaven wants us to say "Please!" when others need His help, whether they be friends or family or those "who are in authority over us."

## Does God Always Answer Our Prayers?

Are all prayers answered the way God answered the prayer for President Bush and the American hostage?

"Only a prayer could save him," a doctor said to me of a dying friend.

I prayed, "Lord, heal him from the cancer that now threatens his life. Heal him, completely and permanently."

He did, but not the way I had *hoped.* The man died hours later.

"The Lord didn't answer your prayer," his grief-stricken wife cried in my arms.

Out of my mouth came a surprising response, not really *my words.* "But he *is* healed. Now! Completely! And permanently! He will never ever again be sick from anything. And we haven't lost him. He's not lost. We know where we can find him." Amen.

❧

It was in one of the deeper, darker times of my life. The decision had been made to build the Crystal Cathedral. The leadoff gift from John Crean for one million dollars had been received.

But the Crystal Cathedral would also need big help from people who lived on small incomes. I believe that God does some of His biggest things through "little" people who love Him and pray.

"How many windows are in the Cathedral?" I asked the architect one day.

"Over ten thousand," he answered.

"What if we 'sold' each window for five hundred dollars at twenty dollars a month for twenty-five months?" I asked. "Almost anyone could help. That would add up to five million."

Across America people responded. Simple, humble, low-income

people like my farming relatives in Iowa. Some famous people responded too, like Frank Sinatra, who bought a window in the name of his mother, who had just died in a plane crash.

In six months almost all the windows were "sold." And names of great people are engraved under each window!

A second gift of one million dollars was promised and would be delivered on the promised date by one of this century's most generous and philanthropic persons, W. Clement Stone.

Success was within our grasp! But then horrific inflation appeared. Estimates projected that if inflation was not brought into line, the cost of the cathedral would increase by another ten million dollars in thirty-six months for a final cost of seventeen million. How could these wild, uncontrollable, unpredicted increases be covered? Would we have to abort the plans with only a hole in the ground?

I was returning from our Australian office when I got a telephone call in Tahiti. It was from our church accountant, Charles Cringle.

"Good news, Bob. Crocker Bank in Los Angeles has agreed to loan us the extra ten million we'll need. The church board met last night, and, pending your approval, agreed enthusiastically to accept it. We'll have the papers ready for you to sign when you get home."

I had been in steady—almost hourly—prayer for weeks, even months, and had never believed we could qualify for a bank loan in the eight-figure bracket! We, who had started this church with two members and five hundred dollars? If I hadn't been working so closely with the Lord, I would have jumped with joy and accepted this line of credit as an answer to prayer.

Instead, I heard myself say, "What's the interest and the terms of the loan, Charles?"

I had been operating this church from day one on a fiscal principle I believe I had received from God in prayer: *Borrow as much as you can, to do as much good as you can, as fast as you can.*

I defined "as much as you can" as the size of the loan you could secure and serve. "Serve" to me meant we would have to at least show enough surplus in operational income to pay the interest on the loan and eliminate the principle in twenty years.

"The terms are very good," my accountant answered. "Interest is 2 percent above the prime rate, which is 9.5 percent today. We don't think it will go much higher," he said. "The payoff will be a minimum of ten years, and they'll consider extending that."

"But Charles, what if interest rises? Even at 9.5 percent plus 2 percent, that's 11.5 percent or $1,150,000 a year for the interest alone! And I don't see that surplus. I don't think we can handle that." I felt in my heart a powerful presence of a spirit that said, *No. Don't do it.*

The board meeting was a chilly experience. I refused to go along and accept the loan.

"Then you can go out and raise the cash," I was told. On that note the meeting ended.

"Help!" I prayed somberly.

It was an almost sleepless night for me. We would need a million in cash in two months to keep the project from shutting down in an embarrassing failure.

Another miracle idea came: "Have a million-dollar offering on a single Sunday next month." A human impossibility.

I prayed.

I had a personal net worth of nothing except the ten-thousand-dollar inheritance I'd received only a few years before from the estate of my father. I had invested it in a small oceanfront apartment that I had bought for $35,000 and used as a private writing studio. I heard that real estate had really soared. I checked. The apartment now had a value of $175,000. I didn't hesitate.

"I'll let my dad make the leadoff gift," I told Arvella. She agreed.

The apartment sold quickly. After the balance of the mortgage was paid, I was able to lay a cashier's check for $150,000 on the boardroom table as the first gift toward a million-dollar special offering.

"Thank you, Dad," I said silently. We raised 1.4 million dollars on one Sunday four weeks later.

Now I knew we'd exhausted the reserves of my congregation. *Where could I go?* I prayed. A name came to mind. Mary Crowley, from Dallas, Texas. We were friends. She was wealthy.

I called. Yes, she'd see me. "Come on over." She had just given a million dollars for a new building at her home church, First Baptist in Dallas, Texas, founded by George Truett. Yes, the same George Truett who had inspired my seminary student mind with a "forty-year" plan—the germ of the idea that God used to get me to California twenty years earlier!

I was met warmly by Mary in her mansion. She shared my excitement about what was happening with our building plans. She was also on Billy Graham's board of directors.

"I'm all for great buildings God can use," she said. That encouraged me, as I was preparing to ask her to make a gift to match John Crean's and W. Clement Stone's. "We are planning a building for Billy Graham on the campus of Wheaton College," she mentioned. "It'll cost a lot too," she said.

"How much?" I asked.

"Probably thirty million," she answered.

"How much have you raised?" I heard myself ask.

"Well, we really haven't gotten that far," she said. She turned and gazed at the beautiful artist's rendering in my hand of the Crystal Cathedral. "Let's pray about this," she said. "Let's go to my private chapel."

She led me outdoors, through her garden, over a rustic bridge, across a stream. There, nestled in her private woods, was a tiny, secluded, charming little chapel. Inside were about a dozen high-backed "prayer chairs."

Mary prayed first for me and my dream.

Then it was my turn. How could I ask God to guide her to help me? Instead I was shocked to hear myself say, "Thank You, Lord, for Mary's wealth, for the gift she gave to her own church. And may she be able and led to make a large leadoff gift for the Billy Graham building on Wheaton's campus."

I rose and said it bluntly, "Mary, I'd like to ask you to give a million dollars to kick off that Billy Graham building."

I saw a look in her eyes that expressed surprise, without any hint of resistance.

"Oh! I've got to catch my plane!" I said. And minutes later I was gone. I had come to pray on Level Two, "Help!" But in my prayer I was shifted by God's Spirit to Level Three, "Please!" I prayed for someone else instead.

Some time later I heard the news.

"Thank you so much, Bob." It was the voice of my friend Billy Graham. "Mary Crowley has just given us a gift of one million dollars. She told me you asked her to make the gift."

I almost shouted aloud with joy. My cry of "Please!" had been heard.

But then I had to settle down. Where would I go now for my needs? Mary Crowley was the last friend I could go to who could possibly make a gift of that size. I needed one million dollars—fast! The contractor had demanded that we deposit another million dollars in the next six weeks or he would have to shut down construction!

Within days, a letter came from a total stranger:

**Dear Dr. Schuller:**

**You don't know me, but I'm one of your *Hour of Power* listeners.**

**I saw and heard about your Crystal Cathedral project underway in California. What is the financial status of this venture?**

**Would another million-dollar gift from a gentleman in Chicago be needed or helpful?**

**It will not be necessary for you to call or come to see me. A letter will do.**

> **Sincerely,**
> **Foster McGaw**

And he listed his private telephone number. I checked out the name. He was for real. He was the founder and president of American Hospital Supply, a major American corporation!

I called Mr. McGaw. "Yes," he wanted me to come.

I went. He and his wife, Mary, heard the story.

"When do you need the cash?" he asked.

"We need to deposit one million in the construction fund by September 14," I answered, "or the contractor will shut down the project. That's two weeks from today."

Foster looked at his wife and said, "Mary, we promised to give that college a million, but they're in no hurry. Let's just write out a check for the Crystal Cathedral today!"

Mary nodded. Foster got up and sat at a little desk where he wrote out the check. He handed it to me, grinning from ear to ear. I was stunned. Tears rolled out of my eyes. Here it was. One million dollars!

Prayer: My soul's *adventure* with God! How often will God wait to give us help on the second level until He sees we are ready to forget our hopes in exchange for bringing someone else's dream or needs into our private, passionate prayer?

Not many months later I was invited by Foster McGaw to attend his eightieth birthday party. There were six of us around the luncheon table at his country club dining room.

I thanked him again. "You know, Foster, I never knew you. God alone motivated you. He wants the Crystal Cathedral paid for when it is finished. God knows we cannot afford to go into debt. Without your cash gift, we would have failed."

He smiled. "The Lord made me able to make money to give money," he said. "I've written out 134 checks for one million dollars! Over thirty colleges have been on the receiving end. Now, since I've been generous and come to my eightieth birthday, I think I have the right to do something to bring me real pleasure on my big birthday."

"Great, Foster," I said, "What would that be, if I may ask?"

"Well, I knew you would ask. So I wrote a little note to explain." He handed me a sealed envelope. "Don't open it now, Reverend. Wait until you're on the plane."

Three hours later I was on the plane returning to Los Angeles. I reached in my pocket, pulled out the letter, and opened it. Inside was another check payable to the Crystal Cathedral building fund for exactly one million dollars.

The Crystal Cathedral opened September 16, 1980. Debt free! It has since become the television "studio" seen by more than twenty million people every week.

It has become the place where nearly one million people a year visit, worship, attend the "Glory of Christmas" and "Glory of Easter" programs, and attend high school graduation ceremonies.

Here governors and presidents have come to worship and to attend packed services for funerals of prestigious people.

No Possibility-Thinking person doubts today that the Crystal Cathedral, only fifteen years old, was an answer to prayer. No cynical atheist, no skeptical journalist, and no critical religious believer would ever be able to explain this successful achievement by leaving prayer and God out of the picture.

I have now lived long enough to prove my critics wrong. And I was right for one simple reason: I prayed for guidance longer and deeper than my critics did. I prayed. They only judged.

Here's the big lesson my soul has learned in this adventure with God: Never openly fault or publicly criticize any person's dreams, desires, or decisions unless you have prayed over the issue as profoundly, passionately, and persistently as they have prayed. Yes, you may question them privately and respectfully. Look. Listen. Think. They may be closer to God's will than you are.

The final cost of the cathedral? Seventeen million dollars—fourteen million in cash on hand and the remaining three million in pledges that would be paid in only a few months.

The business pages that month predicted the past three years of wild inflation had peaked and would pass.

On the day of the grand opening of the debt-free cathedral, the prime interest rate was 22 percent.

Had we taken the ten-million-dollar mortgage, our interest of 2 percent over prime would have cost our church 24 percent or $2,400,000 a year! We would have gone bankrupt! Charles Cringle, our very proper, reserved British accountant—a man not easily given to emotion—and I cried while we thanked our God!

# Chapter 6

# Broken! Then
# Belief Restored!

The Crystal Cathedral was finished. Debt free! But one painful experience still lingered to dampen my joy. A terrible, painful occurrence had erupted when our church board was meeting to see for the first time the architect's model of the proposed Crystal Cathedral. All of us were excited and enthused.

At that time we had nothing! We had borrowed two hundred thousand dollars from Bank of America to hire the architect. We were just managing to pay our bills and had no surplus cash.

"Let's build it!" was the Possibility-Thinking response. I had taught them well. "It will cost seven million? We can borrow all of that through a bond sale," a deacon offered optimistically.

What was an exciting discussion turned into a lengthy debate. Before the issue was voted on, I spoke forthrightly, "I simply cannot go along with a bond sale."

"Then you can go out and raise the millions of dollars yourself, Dr. Schuller. I'm finished!" shouted the rebuffed deacon. He jumped from his corner seat on the sofa, and while his stunned fellow trustees froze in embarrassed silence, he almost ran across the corporate boardroom to the exit and slammed the door behind him.

He was gone. In one horrible moment, one of my dearest friends suddenly, tragically, became a hostile opponent.

It was the single, unmatched, most painful moment in all of my years as chairman of the board. And it had happened so innocently and unpredictably.

The meeting ended with prayer. But ringing in our minds was the deacon's final challenge, "Okay, Dr. Schuller, you go out and raise the money!"

That night was certainly one of the most unsettling ones of my life.

Half a world away, God was preparing someone to help rescue me from my dark night of despair.

In Ireland there lived a young minister who had visited America, where he had attended the Robert Schuller Institute for Successful Church Leadership. He had returned to Ireland, to dangerous, terrorist-plagued Belfast. He was and is a Protestant and could be targeted for an enemy attack. But he had been mentally soaked with Possibility Thinking by this American preacher.

The night of the board meeting, I tossed sleeplessly in my California bed, praying, "Oh, God. Is the dream of a Crystal Cathedral only my vain, egotistical fantasy? Should I walk away from it? Please tell me!" That same night, the Irish minister awoke from a deep sleep. Wide awake, he threw off his bedcovers, got out of bed, and—controlled by an irresistible impulse—prayed. Then he walked to his desk, put a light on, reached for paper and pen, and impulsively wrote a letter to Robert Schuller in America.

Three desperate days passed as I surrendered my dream to God. The disturbing board meeting had been held on Monday night. Next Sunday I would have to say something to the congregation that was waiting for "an important announcement by Robert Schuller." Would I have to dismiss the dream of the Crystal Cathedral?

On Friday, in my mail was a first-class, airmail letter postmarked "Belfast, Ireland." (For the Irish minister's security, I have chosen not to give his name. The rest of the letter is precisely as he wrote it.)

**Dear Dr. Schuller,**

> **I feel that I must write you these words right away.**
> **I was up early this morning talking to the Lord. God**

brought you forcefully to my mind, and I used most of my prayer time standing by you in prayer. Here is what God told me to tell you:

> "Tell him that I love him. Tell him that everything is going to be all right. Tell him not to worry for things *will* work out the way I told him beforehand."

> I have never written a letter like this before to anyone, yet I feel so compelled to mail it to you right away.

> My prayers are with you all the way.

>> **Yours in our Lord, for miracles.**
>> **(Signed)**

I could not believe the words I read! My soul was impacted by what I knew for sure was a direct message from the eternal God who had been answering my childhood prayer all of these years. Now He wanted to give me an incredible church to preach in!

Sunday morning I made the announcement: "I have a dream! An impossible dream! But it has come from God. He has promised, 'If you have faith as a grain of mustard seed you can say to your mountain—"move"—and it will move. And nothing will be impossible to you.' We will build the Crystal Cathedral to the glory of God!" And the people applauded.

Months passed. The million-dollar miracles happened. God knew people I didn't know. He mixed and matched the minds and hearts that transformed the mountain into a miracle.

But the angry deacon stopped coming to church. My hunger for his friendship was left unsatisfied. He rebuffed my invitations. His anger deepened with time.

Months added up to years. Years added up to a decade. We would occasionally appear at the same event. A wedding. A funeral. The hurt never healed.

His wife remained faithful, friendly, helpful, and positively prayerful.

Fifteen years passed. I got a message: The deacon was in the hospital, gravely ill. A stroke? A mysterious infection? They did not know what was wrong. He might live only a few more days or weeks.

"Would he accept me if I came to the hospital to pray for him?" His wife listened to my phone call.

"I think he would," she answered. "Yes, you may call on him. I'll pray for both of you."

I stepped into his private room. There he lay alone. He looked terrible. "May I come in and pray for you?" I asked.

His eyes filled with tears. He struggled and strained to speak. The words were muddled but understandable. "Oh, Bob!" he cried while the tears rolled down. "Oh, Bob, why did I treat you so badly!"

I tried to interrupt, but he could not stop his outpouring of repentant remorse.

"I did a terrible thing to you! Just awful! Awful!"

I opened my arms to hug him. I smiled, tears running down my cheeks too. "It's okay, dear friend. It's all behind us."

We were restored!

Prayer—what an adventure my soul has had with my living God!

# "Spare Him, O Lord"

You and I will never know how many close calls we have had.

All this time—yes, all my life—others have prayed for God's mercy and tender care for me. "Spare him, O Lord, from accidents that might be caused by carelessness or mistakes. Spare him from death that would come too soon, before he can live out and fulfill Your fruitful plan for his life."

On February 15, 1995, at 5:00 P.M., NBC television news in Los Angeles broke the story. It would never have been reported if the husband of an on-camera news reporter from NBC had not been on that flight! He was Mike Nason, and he was sitting with me as he telephoned his wife. Later, the story was picked up by the leading newspapers in California.

"A near air collision happened over Los Angeles, California, this afternoon. On board the United flight was Dr. Robert Schuller. Ground radio interference caused the live communication to be broken off between the air traffic controllers and the pilot of the wide-body plane that was descending and preparing to land after a nonstop flight from Washington, D.C. At an elevation of 3,800 feet, the airline collision warning system flashed in the cockpit. The pilot responded, and the aircraft rose sharp and fast, angling to the right. A collision course with a small private plane that had just left the Long Beach Airport was avoided."

How many thousands of prayers were logged for everyone on that plane—including me—by parents, grandparents, children, and friends of the passengers?

Where would any of us be if it were not for the thousands of prayers prayed for God's watchful care over our lives? And what about the prayers for our children? Each day, before the night falls, my wife and I pray for our five children, their spouses, and our seventeen grandchildren! That's our commitment. We pray for each one by name (that's twenty-seven names in all) that God will protect them "from accident and injury, sin and sickness," that they may live a long life blessed by a loving God.

## Saved from Death Again and Again

I'll say it again. You and I will never know how many close calls we have had.

Germs that died after we were unknowingly exposed.

Faulty parts in airplanes and cars that came so close to breaking down in what would have been—unknown to us—the end of our lives.

When I was ten years old, I was carrying a pail filled with eggs. Two huge horses were nuzzling their necks together in the middle of the yard. And I decided to walk between them to "break up their little party."

The next thing I knew I was walloped by the legs of one of the horses kicking me in my face. I was lifted from the ground and thrown down. The pail of eggs scattered in broken pieces of white and yellow around the yard. My chin was cut open. Look at me carefully today and you can see the scar as it grows deeper with every passing year.

I have often thought when I shave myself, *Now if that horse's hoof had been about three or four inches higher it could have fractured my skull. And I would have died young.* Whose prayers were covering me that day? Was it my own childhood prayer, "Make me a preacher when I grow up"? After all, God would have to keep me alive before He could make me a preacher!

Then there was the Sunday morning in 1968 when I was nearly electrocuted in church. The pulpit of the sanctuary had a built-in bookstand twelve inches wide and nearly four feet long. It was long enough for the preacher to spread out several sheets of notes, and it stood next to the sliding glass walls that, when opened, allowed me to stand in the open space and look directly at persons worshiping in their cars in the drive-in church parking lot.

I would walk to this high pulpit and pick up the microphone that was connected into the sound system. Built flush into the podium edge was a long fluorescent tube, hidden by a piece of frosted glass.

Unknown to anyone, the two thin electrical wires within the tube had broken, and now, because of an electrical short, that Sunday morning when the light was turned on, electricity would surge through that book rest. Of course, no one would feel it—unless they were grounded.

As I stepped into the pulpit to announce the beginning of the service, I held in my right hand the microphone that would ground me. When I placed my left hand on the charged book rest, six hundred volts of electricity entered my body through my left hand, freezing the microphone in my right hand. I could not release my grip on the grounded microphone. The charge lifted my two-hundred-pound body at least six inches and hurled me backward onto the floor. The sound cord was providentially behind me, so when I fell, the weight of my body hit it, pulling the microphone from my right hand and releasing me from the pulsating, shocking currents of electricity.

Many in the audience thought I'd been shot. (Martin Luther King had just been assassinated.)

I did not lose consciousness. I rose, smoothed my robe, picked up the mike and, standing three feet from the smoking bookstand, I smiled and said, "I want you to know I'm really 'charged up' to preach this morning. I've never felt so 'bright' as I do today." We all laughed.

Electricians later showed me the "freak" accidental breakage and burnout in the tube.

Then there was the time I might have been stabbed to death on the sidewalk in Amsterdam!

Three men approached me as I walked only a block from my hotel. Two of the three were suddenly in front of me to block my escape. The third stood right behind me, put his left arm around my neck, and squeezed tightly. "I have an open knife in my hand. It's going right into your belly unless you give me your money and your wristwatch. Now! Fast!"

Even though it was a crowded sidewalk and broad daylight, no one knew I was being held up. I had the sense not to shout, fearing for my life. The mugger's left hand felt a gold chain that held a solid gold medal around my neck. As I reached to hand over to him my paper currency, I felt him pull the gold chain.

"Stop! I'll give it to you," I offered, protecting my neck from a ripping chain. I handed him the chain and the gold medal I had been wearing every Sunday on my robe. The medallion was a bas-relief of the Crystal Cathedral's Good Shepherd statue on one side, with the Possibility Thinker's Creed on the other. He grabbed it, along with my cash.

I waited for the plunge of the knife, but suddenly he was gone! Around the corner and out of sight!

Who prayed for me that day? Will I ever know whose prayers saved my life?

Three weeks later I came within a hair's breadth of drowning in the Pacific Ocean.

I was invited to fish for marlin off of Cabo San Lucas in Mexico. The rental boat, though old, seemed sturdy enough. But the waves began to build to white caps with heavy swells.

"Maybe we should go in," I suggested. Only moments later, the ocean turned rough and wild. I was standing with feet spread to ride the bouncing boat, which was tossing like a bronco in a rodeo, when a huge wave hit the side and hurled me off my feet. I flew across the open rear deck, where I hit the side rail, knocking out a two-foot section. I somehow grabbed a rope attached to the stern.

Lying flat on the deck, my head and shoulders were already off the boat, and I was staring down on churning waters. I was saved from going overboard by the single rope I clutched in my right hand.

Within seconds I felt the crew members pulling me by my legs onto the open deck. They saved my life.

"We couldn't have gone in after you," one said later. "No one could swim in that sea!"

That—for sure—was a close call. What prayer, prayed by whom, saved my life *that* day?

Was it a close call during my college years when my family drove ninety miles an hour to escape a tornado bearing down on us in a wild cloud of deadly dust?

Years later, it *was* a close call when a hundred-year-old tree was torn from its roots and crashed into the porch outside the room where I was sleeping.

"If it had fallen only a few feet north, it would have crashed through the large window right where your bed was and killed you!" one of my relatives said.

How often has God spared your life? How close have you come to disaster?

Your car is traveling at sixty-five miles an hour in heavy freeway traffic. Another car races toward you at the same speed. A head-on collision is avoided by only the three feet that separates the two lanes. The yellow lines kept you apart? Yes, as they have thousands of times. But how often was the approaching car driven by someone under the influence of chemicals or alcohol? You and I will never know.

I only know that I'm alive today. And I surely know that there's never been a day in which someone, somewhere, has not covered and cradled me safely in prayer.

Amen! Hallelujah!

# An Eye That Never Closes

I was booked to deliver a management address at a national sales conference in Las Vegas. The commitment had been made months before. I learned that Billy Graham had scheduled an evangelism event that same night, and for extended nights, in the same city. My office called his office to see if I could connect with him while we were both in town.

"Tell Bob," Billy replied, "I'd love to have him stay over a night and join me on the platform."

I accepted.

When my traveling companion and I arrived, we were met graciously by one of Billy's aides, who surprised us with this announcement: "Dr. Schuller, you are booked at the MGM Hotel. I know that's where you always stay when you come to town, but Billy and his staff are staying at the Hilton. It's right next to the Convention Center, so they can walk over and avoid the heavy traffic. So Billy has taken the liberty to book you a room in the Hilton. Okay? We were sure you'd be happy with this, so we canceled your reservation at the MGM Grand Hotel for tonight."

"No problem." Gratitude for Billy's generosity overrode my preference to stay at a familiar and favorite hotel—the MGM Grand.

My lecture that night went well. Afterward, my aide, Mike Nason, escorted me to my room.

"I'll knock at your door around 8:00 A.M. tomorrow, Bob, and we'll go have breakfast," he said.

On schedule, the knock on the door came the next morning. Mike and I walked to the elevator. Large picture windows next to the elevator waiting area framed perfectly the MGM Hotel only a few blocks away.

While we waited for the elevator to reach our twentieth floor, Mike pointed to the MGM and said, "I wonder what room we would have had there last night. For sure they'd have reserved good ones. They always do."

"Mike, look. Smoke. Are they allowed to burn litter in the daytime here in Las Vegas?" We weren't allowed to build such fires in Los Angeles. A heavy, rising column of black smoke was curling and twisting from the ground high into the sky.

Before our elevator arrived, and before Mike could answer, we saw orange flames break out of the smoke. "The MGM is on fire!" Mike said.

Now we could see flashing red lights of police cars and fire engines. We stood transfixed with a spectacular view of the horrible drama unfolding. People appeared on balconies. One lowered a rope made from sheets, hoping to escape. Helicopters came, two, then three of them landing on the roof to remove hotel guests. At least one person leaped from a balcony.

Smoke billowed now from many places on the side of the hotel. Ambulances roared to the scene. From our twentieth floor lookout we could see traffic on the main streets stretching for over a mile. Red lights flashed from emergency vehicles. Police cars, fire trucks, ambulances all mixed with the heavy morning traffic.

"We were supposed to have been in there, Mike, right now!"

More than one hundred people died or were injured in that fire. I stood there watching the tragic event and praying for the people trapped inside the hotel. It was the first and only time I have seen human beings on balconies desperately waving for someone to come to their rescue with a rope or ladder.

I could have died in that fire. If Billy Graham had not canceled my reservations, I would have been in that burning hotel.

# On the Receiving End of Countless Prayers

Yes, I have had my share of close calls, dangerous moments when I was protected or pulled from the edge of disaster by the power of prayer. But the greatest miracle of my life brought by intercessory prayer happened only a few years ago. And it all started with an innocent bump on the head.

I was in Amsterdam, visiting our ministry's office there, preparing to fly to Rome the next day for a private meeting with Pope John Paul II.

After arriving in Amsterdam, I stepped into our car and banged the side of my head on the door frame. The bump hurt for a few minutes, but I soon forgot about it.

Later I had a headache. I thought I might have some "bug," so I took four aspirin and went to bed early. I didn't want to miss the meeting with the Pope the next day.

A combination of a strong heart, thinned blood (four aspirin will do it!), and a Do Not Disturb sign I had placed on my front door spelled disaster when the broken blood vessel in my head poured blood into my skull. If a blood vessel breaks, it leaks—unless it's in the skull. That "container" does not have a spout. When it's full— well, that's it.

For nearly ten hours I was in my hotel room. They found me in a coma on the balcony. I do not recall going out there. I was unclothed. When my body fell backward, it came to rest against the door leading to the balcony and served as a two-hundred-pound weight that prevented my rescuers from opening the glass door from the inside.

God was in this too. Had my comatose body fallen forward instead of backward, it would have hurtled over the low balcony railing and into the canal, thirty feet below. Death would have been by drowning.

"Is he dead?" my son-in-law, Paul David Dunn, asked. A hotel bellman rushed for a ladder and from an adjoining balcony laid the ladder flat to make a bridge. Rung by rung, he carefully made his way to my balcony.

"He's alive, I think!" he answered, pulling my body away from the door. My two aides, near panic, covered me with a blanket.

The ambulance driver would have a conflict with the head of my Dutch office, Joop Post, who was riding in the front seat with him. My son-in-law was riding with my wounded, comatose body in the back.

"We'll take him to the closest medical center," the ambulance driver said.

"Listen to me!" Joop interrupted. "You will go directly to the Amsterdam University Hospital!"

"No!" the driver protested. "By law we are required to take a patient to the *closest* medical center. The University Hospital is much farther!"

Only a year before, Joop had had a serious heart condition. He was taken to the "closest medical center." There, much precious time was lost in preliminary check-in and examination before the seriousness of his case was confirmed. He was then sent immediately to the University Hospital, where the best care and equipment were available.

Remembering that incident from only a year before, Joop threatened to take over the driving of the ambulance. Under this threat, the driver turned left at the light and with siren wailing headed straight for the Amsterdam University Hospital.

Joop probably kept me from being dead on arrival.

"I estimate you had only twenty minutes left when you got here," the chief neurosurgeon would tell me one year later when I returned to Amsterdam to thank him. I prayed with him. "God, thank you for these ten fingers that scalped me, drilled through the bone, and went into my brain to stop the bleeding and empty the pool of blood that was about to drown me."

I, of course, never even knew anything was wrong when I passed out ten hours before surgery. Arvella received a call in California. She called our son, Robert, who would accompany her to Amsterdam.

Meanwhile, friends gathered at the Crystal Cathedral to pray around the clock for my healing.

Was it hours or days later when I awoke? I didn't know where I was, except that it was a hospital room with a nurse looking down at me. I didn't know why I was there or what had happened. I didn't know that I had had brain surgery, that for ten hours my brain had been invaded by a rising flood of blood. I had no idea that I stumbled onto a balcony, that I had been saved by Joop from time-wasting bureaucracies in state hospitals, that I had all my hair shaved, that they had completely peeled the skin from my skull. I didn't know that the doctors had drilled through my head and lifted the top of my skull the way you cut the top of a pumpkin to make a jack-o'-lantern. Or that they had then entered the brain, stopped the bleeding, replaced the bony cap, and hoped for the best.

"We don't know," the doctor said to Arvella in response to her question about my condition. "He may have lost his memory. We'll just have to pray. He will live. We have saved his life. It was very close, I must tell you. He had been bleeding far too long. Had this not happened in the nighttime, they'd have spotted it much sooner.

"Mrs. Schuller, your husband was very near death. But that's behind us. But we can't tell when we go into a brain what we have touched or what temporary or permanent damage has been done. He is sixty-five years old. He has a very strong heart and a very healthy body. He could live another thirty years. But—his brain? We don't know."

While the doctor was talking with my wife, I was having my first visitor—my heavenly Father—the God who had heard my father's prayer, had given him another son late in his wife's childbearing years, brought me into this world, and had sent Uncle Henry to deliver a special message to me early in life so I'd never waste time trying to know what I should do.

Yes, this God, who had set things up for me—family, school, Christian education, wife—so that I could be a preacher when I grew up, He was my first visitor.

Before I regained consciousness, He communicated these words, which consumed me with sheer spiritual excitement. As a writer and speaker who had been enjoying the gift of the Holy Spirit for more than thirty years, I had come to know, to recognize, and to respect most profoundly the messages that come through my "inner ear." Sentences like "Tough times never last—but tough people do," and "Success is never ending—failure is never final," and "Life's not fair—but God is good."

Now, in the moment before I would awaken from what had been nearly fourteen hours of a coma sleep and surgery, God wanted to make sure I had the right mental attitude. He gave me what only He could give. He supplied His healing power as only He could do it. He gave me, once more, a great gift—*vision for the future.* As my eyes opened, this God-given sentence was *there*—in my mind:

**How sweet it is to stand on the edge of tomorrow.**

I woke up with this powerful sentence completely consuming my attention and dominating my mind! I didn't care or wonder where I was or why I was there.

I gave the nurse an urgent message: "Please, a pen and paper!" I could so easily lose the words. I intensely repeated them over and over and over. As a writer, I knew how easily the gift of a stunning phrase could be lost.

But I didn't realize that I was not making intelligible words as the garbled sounds of my request tumbled from my bandaged head.

"Give him a pen and paper," my wife said to the nurse. Arvella could not make sense of my mumbling either.

I grabbed the pen and put it to the paper.

I tried to write the words I was relishing as a "get well gift, better than flowers" from my Creator and Friend. I scrawled the words, "How sweet it is to stand on the edge of tomorrow."

Arvella couldn't make it out. The only signal my brain sent my hand resulted in a scratched line.

The next day, I tried to write the sentence again. I couldn't even shape a letter, just a jagged line!

And the next day, again.

"My husband is a professional writer. When will he be able to write?" she asked the doctor.

"We have no idea, Mrs. Schuller."

"Will he ever be able to speak again?" she asked.

"Mrs. Schuller, we don't know. He is not getting better. We have to go in for another surgery. And he needs a blood transfusion."

So God sent her a message, not with words, but with *wings*.

Staring over my body, she noticed suddenly, outside the window, a sparrow fluttering its wings, hovering its friendly body. There! Where there was no branch, no window sill, where there was no rhyme or reason for a sparrow to come and remain too long, flapping its wings. This was the powerful thought that came into my wife's anxious mind:

**God, who watches the little sparrow, is watching over your husband. Your husband is of more value than this little bird. He will be well.**

I was silent, sleeping. Dreaming the words. Listening to God whisper to me the gift that He was giving me to share with the world.

**How sweet it is to stand on the edge of tomorrow.**

What an adventure God and my soul were in together! Just the two of us.

## "God Is All Over Him"

"Mrs. Schuller, you have a visitor," the nurse quietly informed my wife. It was John Wimber, my friend, a world-renowned minister and a neighboring pastor from California. John "happened" to be teaching in Holland.

John's special ministry is prayer—"signs and wonders." He believes it. He practices it. His ministry focuses on prayers for miraculous healings.

"Some are healed. Others are not," he teaches. "We don't know why. But we believe in the power of prayer."

My wife welcomed John and his wife, Carol. In a deep sleep, a semicomatose condition, I never knew these visitors were there. John stepped up to the edge of my bed. My head was no longer bandaged, but it was cleanly shaved, with a deep red circle of stitches encircling the scalp. John, Carol, and Arvella encircled my bed. John extended his palms above my body. Before he could speak, his hands began to quiver, then tremble, then shake.

"I feel the invisible presence of God coming from his wounded body," John said. "God is all over him."

Now I was ready for my second brain surgery, only eight days later. It was a success.

I opened my eyes. I saw Arvella. My face was all she could see. The rest of my head was wrapped in white bandages.

I think I smiled!

I know I spoke. A few days later, the words came out clearly:

*How sweet it is to stand on the edge of tomorrow.*

Amen.

# GOD, LET'S CONNECT

*Two-way prayer works wonders!*

"FOR ALL THE PROMISES OF GOD IN HIM ARE YES."
— 2 CORINTHIANS 1:20 —

# Chapter 7

# Heart to Heart

In the Broadway musical *1776,* a scene opens with John Adams crying out:

*"Is anybody there?"*
*"Does anybody care?"*
*"Does anybody see what I see?"*

Prayer is a soul's adventure that sets out with the ultimate assumption:

*Someone is out there.*
*He is a lot more than I am.*
*He really cares!*
*He can and will listen.*

Everything that's great starts with an idea. God will give me a dream! An impossible dream. Always, Level One. *His* dreams are impossible dreams waiting to be turned into possible dreams. And always these impossible dreams stimulate enough passion to motivate the egotistical soul to humility and to cry for "Help!"—Level Two.

On Level Three you find your prayer life is moving on and up to a higher level. You are learning the joy and value of unselfish living, forgetting yourself and unselfishly thinking and praying for some-one else!

Are you ready for an exciting personal encounter on your soul's adventure with God? That's Level Four!

On this level you don't want your own way. You just don't want to make a mistake! You're not ego driven—you're success oriented. You just want to know the right thing to do. You don't want to fail! You pray that you will choose your failures carefully! So when and where you do fail, it will not hurt you! "I chose to fail at golf—so I'd have the time to succeed in building the church," I have often said.

You're a truly humble person. You're purged of self-delusions, blinding pride, and foolish arrogance. On this fourth level your sole desire is to become the person God wants you to be. Guidance— *divine guidance*—is what you seek with a passion. Now you pray for God to help you set your priorities and goals wisely.

You now admit that you're increasingly sure that not all of your answers are totally right. You're set up emotionally and spiritually to be shaped, changed, and molded, to be receptive to divine inspirations that can help, encourage, correct, enlighten, or affirm. You're ready to step into the holy presence of the Almighty for an honest-to-God, heart-to-heart talk.

Another way to describe this level is "Two-Way Prayer." You enter the "holy of holies," not asking for possessions, property, power, or position—for yourself or for anyone else.

You only seek enlightenment.

You come trusting that God has the answers to the questions you cannot and must not avoid asking. Your prejudices and preconceptions are left behind. You come to learn the truth.

He has wanted you to get in this mood. The two of you can now relate. Here He can touch you when and where and how He knows you need it most.

## Jesus Christ: Number One Hero!

That first childhood prayer of mine—"Make me a preacher when I grow up"—was on Levels One and Two. Well and good.

Now seminary was finished. I took a call—my first church—in a Chicago suburb. The city was, I believed, large enough to keep me busy for forty years. There were thirty-three members in this my first church. This was small and challenging enough to become my "George Truett Church."

I really didn't question the Lord. I simply went with my new wife of one week to begin what I thought would be a forty-year project.

Here God would begin to sharpen His servant. And while He dealt with my academic pride and youthful arrogance, He would also startle me in an incredible "mountaintop" encounter.

I was given a salary of two hundred dollars per month, enough so I could afford to walk three blocks each morning to a little bakery and bring to my wife's breakfast table sweet rolls and doughnuts— warm, fresh, sweet.

The little church grew, but primarily when Christians from other churches came and joined. I wanted new converts. I was failing, and down deep I knew it. Unchurched persons who didn't believe in the Bible or in Jesus Christ didn't want to hear heavy, Calvinistic sermons. My words didn't touch them where they were hurting.

"Pride comes before the fall." The Bible says that, and I would experience it. I was a proud young minister, with my education being the taproot of an intellectual, elitist conceit.

My B.A. degree was from Hope College, which had just been ranked in the top ten colleges and universities in America. I just knew I was *really* well educated.

My three years of graduate studies at Western Theological Seminary had also been a "heady" intellectual experience. At that time and place I was certain that the greatest theologian in history was the French lawyer who became a founding father of Protestantism—John Calvin. His flagship theological work was an imposing four-volume set called *Institutes of the Christian Religion.*

In my first months at seminary I was introduced to these heavy-weight books, and I studied them with passion. I learned how in the sixteenth century, Calvin's thought was the theological foundation for most of Protestantism. The Reformed Church in the Netherlands, from which my blood family all came; the Presbyterian Church, originally called "The Reformed Church in Scotland"; and the Anglican-Protestant Church in England and the British Isles—all were shaped and soaked in Calvinism.

A century later, in the 1700s, a godly leader named John Wesley would be forced out of the Church of England because he was not "Calvinistic enough." He focused on the individual's freedom to decide. "You," he said, "are a person, and your life is not predestined—you are an individual, and you must make your own decisions." I was taught that Wesley's view was wrong. Calvin was right. We are creatures of destiny—not personal decisions. Years later I would see both are right! We are destined to be decision makers.

The Methodist Church was born, and in the two hundred years from Wesley's time to Schuller's time, Methodism became the fastest-growing branch of Protestantism.

But I was Dutch Reformed. I looked down on Methodists.

"You mean there's no topical or scriptural index to John Calvin's *Institutes?*" I asked my theology professor in seminary. I couldn't believe it. It had never been done. "If I were to make an exhaustive index, topical and scriptural, of all four books, would that qualify as a project for my thesis?" I asked. The faculty considered and agreed.

I made the commitment, once again making the decision before I solved the problems.

It would take me three years. I would read every word of all four volumes ten times and finally finish with more than two hundred pages bound in leather and approved by my faculty committee.

I was proud of it. I considered myself, in my youthful naïveté, "unsurpassed as a student of Calvinism in the whole world."

I had also learned to think and reason as a "lawyer" (John Calvin) thought and reasoned. My youthful mind was sharpened in its analytical and critical corners.

As a young preacher my heavy, Calvinistic sermons thrilled Christians from Calvinistic and Reformed Church backgrounds. They bored Methodists, who dropped in and then left, never to return.

I could feel I was missing the mark in wanting to impress and impact non-Christians. Reaching the hearts of unbelievers was where, I would learn later, John Wesley was gifted. God had to humble me and soften and shape my soul. Here is how He did it.

First, somehow I got on the mailing list of Norman Vincent Peale. That was OK. He was the pastor of the oldest and largest Reformed Church in America. Interestingly, he was the son of a Methodist minister, educated at a Methodist seminary, and served a Methodist church until he was called by the dying, old (it dated back to 1628) Marble Collegiate Church at 29th Street and Fifth Avenue in New York City.

Here Peale came in his early thirties. The Depression raged. People were committing suicide in their financial distress.

"God lives, God loves, God listens to *you*," Dr. Peale preached. He preached a helpful Christianity focused on a prayer-hearing, prayer-answering God.

Each month I received printed copies of Dr. Peale's sermons. Each was simple, made up of true stories of how Christ loves and touches people who accept Him. No theology, no heavy messages about total depravity.

I read the titles only: "Hope for Hurting Hearts," "Faith Can Strengthen Your Life," "Real Prayer Really Works," "Change Your Thinking and Your World Will Change." I flipped through the pages. I saw no profound sentences to challenge the "intellectual" mind of this young Calvinist, so I dumped them in my wastebasket.

But the titles went—without my intention, approval, or knowledge—into my subconscious, unfiltered memory system. Here they collected and waited.

Two years later I was failing, and I knew it. In a time of discouragement and depression I would cry out to God, "What am I doing wrong?" And these sermon titles would come marching out of my memory into my conscious mind and give me hope! They caused me to refocus totally my theological priorities. They did not cause me to reject truths in Scripture taught by John Calvin. But Calvin*ism?* "Isms" are interpretations of the writings of the founder. Those hopeful, caring titles purged my Calvinism of a lot of negativity, and I was on a new track.

I had become a "Calvinistic Methodist," but I never really thought of calling myself this until 1993, more than forty years later, when Richard Nixon made his last trip through Russia. He returned home only a few months before his death. His office called and reported, "Every leader I met in Russia, without exception, asked me, 'Mr. Nixon, do you know this Methodist minister named Robert Schuller, whom we see each week on television here in Russia?'"

It actually took me four years in that little Chicago church to be turned into a positive Christian preacher. I experienced a profound paradigm shift because of one book, *Ride the Wild Horses* by J. Wallace Hamilton. It probably did more than any other single book to make me look for the positive in negative situations. It fit beautifully into my Calvinism, even though Hamilton was a Methodist!

Then came the books of E. Stanley Jones, another Methodist. He brilliantly synchronized historical, evangelical, biblical Christian truth with psychology and focused on the needs and hurts of the *individual.*

My sermons changed to become true stories of hurting people whose lives had been saved by faith, hope, and love. And Jesus Christ became my number one, living, loving, lifting hero! My Savior became my best friend. I talked to Him. I was sure He was listening.

My soul really was on an adventure with God!

## A Mountaintop Encounter

December 1954. My Chicago telephone rang. It was a Reformed Church minister, Dr. Raymond Beckering, calling from Los Angeles, California.

"Bob, today The Reformed Church met and decided to start a new church in Garden Grove, California. They want to invite you to come and start it. There are no Reformed people that we know of in the area.

"You and your wife will be the only members. Your salary, two hundred dollars a month, will be paid by our board in New York City. Mrs. Norman Vincent Peale heads that board, and they have promised to pay your salary for one year. You've just got to come here and look over the area."

I was just becoming a "known" and "sought after" young preacher. All I could remember was what Dr. Beckering had told me when I was getting ready to graduate four years before: "California? It's nice, but it just doesn't have any great churches."

Now, four years later, he's asking me to go there? To nothing? To be forgotten by all the larger churches who were beginning to notice me? I had just turned down an invitation to go to an Illinois church that promised good buildings, a great parsonage, prestigious members, and a salary of four hundred dollars a month!

I prayed.

I called one of my members who worked for the Santa Fe Railroad. Could he help me travel to California? "Sure," he said. "I can get you a round-trip ticket, free, with an upper berth to sleep in. Go on. Check it out."

I accepted. I arrived in Garden Grove. Smoke hung thickly about the city. "They're burning orange trees to make room for new houses," someone told me.

"And that fire?" I pointed to another cloud of smoke.

"That's the doing of Walt Disney. He's building a big park. It will open next year."

I was concerned about the low salary. We had a four-year-old daughter, Sheila, and a baby boy, Robert.

I recalled Robert's birth just two months before. "You have your son," the doctor had said as he came out of the delivery room. I turned to the window so he would not see my tears—of joy but also of sadness. The way he said it, *"You have your son,"* I knew this baby would be our only male child. I just knew it.

Now go to California? On only two hundred dollars a month? How could I possibly afford college education for these two children? Salaries would be raised very, very slowly in Dutch Reformed churches. And I would not be allowed to take second jobs. And in those days, a pastor's wife was expected to be her husband's full-time helper at no salary. I would be allowed to give speeches and write books. Dr. Peale did that. But I remembered what my professor had said after I failed the English course: "Don't try to write—stick to preaching."

On the train, coming home from California to Chicago, I climbed alone into my upper berth, drew the drapes, and fell asleep talking to God. It would be my first, really sincere, two-way prayer.

"God, what must I do? Can this be the right move?" I asked.

I listened. I waited. No answer. I fell asleep.

The answer came clearly, surely, in a strange, strange way. The train jerked. Cars jolted. I was awakened. What had happened? Where was I?

I opened the drapes. It was the middle of the night. We were stopped, high on a mountaintop in Arizona. There was a spectacle of serene white beauty such as my youthful eyes had never before seen. It was heavenly! Huge pine trees were draped in deep, white, freshly-fallen snow, and a full moon bathed the midnight scene.

Suddenly, just outside my window, a large deer appeared. A regal buck with large horns on his head. He stared at the train. I stared at him. He abruptly turned. With a white puff of a tail facing me, he leaped. I watched him bound off. His hooves made black holes and powdering puffs of white as he ran.

Then into my mind it came. Unsolicited. Provoked by the majestic image of the deer standing in the pure, white, untouched open forest. It was a message strong and clear and certain: *The greatest churches in the world haven't been organized yet.* It was God's special answer to my prayer.

I knew what I had to do. We would move to California. We would organize a new church in a vast, "untouched," open territory.

છે

God lives. God listens. God loves. God leads.

On that shining, white, moonlit mountaintop in Arizona, I longed only to know: "Dear God, what do You want me to do?"

I desperately needed to know *His* agenda. We needed to have a heart-to-heart talk. I asked. I waited. I slept, and I was awakened. He answered!

While I was listening to God's promise on the mountaintop in Arizona, God was calling a young Buddhist, half a world away, to become a Christian. He was a young teenage boy in Korea. He was not a Christian or even religious.

He would nearly die from tuberculosis. He would cry out to the sky, "Help! God, are You there? Can You heal me?" The miracle happened. He was instantly healed.

"Where can I learn more about God?" he asked.

"You need to talk to a missionary," he was told, and he was pointed to an American missionary whose sister would become an early member of my new California church.

He would become a Christian minister and begin what would become the largest Christian church in the whole world. We would become, in the unfolding years, dear friends.

His name? David Yonggi Cho. On a recent occasion, he called together more than one million members in one place and at one time for a massive prayer rally! And I had the honor of speaking at that gathering!

*The greatest churches in the world haven't been organized yet.* What a powerful prophetic message that was!

# Chapter 8

# The Greatest Positive Thinker Alive

N one of us knows when we will desperately need deep, divine insight and intervention. But we will. Ready to pursue God's dream in California, I would soon find this out.

When the train arrived in Chicago from California, Arvella was waiting.

"I could see it in your face. I knew we would be going to California," she said.

We drove across the states. It was winter. We stopped in Sioux City, Iowa, at a music store run by a friend.

"I'm going to California to start a church," I told him. "My church gave us a farewell gift of three hundred dollars. Is that enough to make a down payment on an electric organ? I married the organist," I said, laughing.

"I have one for $1,800," he answered.

I bought it then and there and trusted my little income could squeeze out the monthly payments. It did.

❧

One month later, we lined up a drive-in theater. We were on our way.

I rang doorbells inviting neighboring suburbanites to come. Nobody was interested in a Reformed Church. So I named it "Garden Grove Community Church."

One young wife answered her door. "I have no religion. My father was Jewish. My mother Catholic. They told me to pick my own religion. Now I've graduated from Stanford, and I'm married. I'm interested. What's your religion?"

"Well," I answered. "As you know in the Old Testament . . ."

She interrupted, "What's that?"

"Well," I began, shocked that a university graduate didn't know, "the Bible is made up of two books—the Old Testament and the New Testament." She interrupted again. "Your religion has two Bibles?"

"Forget it," I said, "just come to church, and if you like it and it helps you, come back."

God was telling me something. These unchurched Californians didn't know the Bible, and they weren't impressed if I quoted the Bible.

I'd have to preach Bible truths but in simple words and simple messages, like Norman Vincent Peale did. No heavy Calvinism. No heavy Bible. Just inspiring, biblical, Christ-centered, spiritual truth to bring them from doubt to faith!

How could I get unchurched people to come to our church in the drive-in theater? I knew they were talking about the number one best-selling book in America according to the *New York Times*. The book: *The Power of Positive Thinking*. The author: Norman Vincent Peale. Yes, surely these people would come to hear *him* speak.

I wrote him a letter. "Come and speak for me, Dr. Peale. I've got a parking lot for 1,700 cars."

He accepted. The momentous Sunday arrived, and it was a sight to see! The place was packed, and an overflow of cars lined the streets. What a crowd!

We sat on folding chairs on the snack bar rooftop. The sun was hot. It was time for me to introduce Dr. Peale. I forgot—in the excitement—to take his bio sheet. I prayed silently, *What do I say, Lord?* Two-way prayer! I listened. God answered.

Out of my mouth came these unthought-of words: "Ladies and gentlemen. We have with us this morning—live and in person—the greatest Positive Thinker in the world today. His name is a household word. His words? Many of us have been inspired by them. If you get to meet him personally and know him as a friend like I do, you'll never be the same. His name? The greatest Positive Thinker alive today—Jesus Christ. And here to tell us all about him is Norman Vincent Peale."

As Dr. Peale rose to speak, he whispered, "Pray for me."

I did, and his message would forever change my own sermons in style, substance, and spirit.

"If Jesus Christ could speak to you now, what would he say to you?" Dr. Peale began. "Would He tell you what sinners you all are?"

Yes! Yes! I nodded. As a Calvinist just becoming a Methodist, I was sure I knew the answer.

"Would He tell you how hellish life is without God?"

Again I was sure I knew the answer.

Peale paused. He paced. Then he bellowed. "No! I don't think that's what Jesus would tell you. Deep, deep, deep down in your heart you already know that! He'd say, 'Follow me, and I will give you *life*— abundantly and eternally!'"

Wow! At the age of twenty-nine I learned a primary lesson in positive preaching to unchurched people!

## Can You Remove This Demonic Fear?

Nothing would ever be the same again—for me or my little church. New members by the hundreds came. Yes, they'd be taught the Bible in classes, where I would go over the classic two-thousand-year-old Christian faith as held by Protestants and Roman Catholics in the Apostles' Creed. But my Sunday sermons were full of the hope and love of God.

I was overwhelmed with work. A thoughtful elder in our church wanted to help me. One day his doorbell rang. It was a brush salesmen. They talked. The salesman was a fresh seminary graduate who couldn't find a job as a minister. The elder knew about my workload and promptly offered him a job as my assistant. Just like that! I had no choice. The church board accepted him without my approval. He was as different from me as night from day.

His theology was centered on sin, hell, the devil, and an angry, wrathful God. He was sure that "Positive Thinking" was from Satan. Peale was a spokesman for the devil. I was in for trouble. Big trouble!

He held secret meetings with members to "get Schuller kicked out." Rumors spread. I knew of the conspiracy. The stress was threatening my soul. Someone gave me a copy of a *Life* magazine cover that read "Ministers Are Cracking Up." The inside story was depressing. Good, educated ministers across the country were having nervous breakdowns. "We never thought it could happen to us," was the usual reaction of these strong men.

That's when the destructive—almost demonic—spirit assailed me. I tried to analyze my stress. Here's how I saw the unfolding dark drama now encircling me:

- **One year ago I began to have the dream of building a walk-in, drive-in church. It would be the first of its kind. Risky.**
- **Two months later, Dr. Peale would preach in the drive-in theater. I had visited him that Sunday afternoon in his room at the Beverly Hilton. I drew my mental picture of my "dream" church for him. "It will be a church where the outside garden flows into the church. Fountains, flowers, trees, sky. Here people could sit inside or in their cars outside. I would be able to push a button, and the side walls would slide open. I could see people in their cars—the handicapped, the celebrities who want privacy." I was so enthused. He was blown away.**

    **"Keep dreaming, Bob. And give the dream time to *evolve*." He rolled out that last word.**
- **Three months later I preached for Dr. Peale at his church, the Marble Collegiate in New York. I was ushered into his private study to robe and pray. On the wall I saw a calendar. On the calendar, a slogan. It was planned by God to be the special strength He knew my adventuring soul would need, for I was beginning to be consumed by a dream, a dream I knew was impossible.**

    **I had only shared the secret with Peale in private.**

Now I was thinking about exposing my dream to the whole congregation. But the prospect of failure was looming so realistically, I was petrified.

It would be easy and safe to keep quiet and abort the wild dream. I was tempted to surrender leadership of my life and God's church to Schuller's fear of failure. Then and there, alone with God in Dr. Peale's office, I read the slogan on the calendar. It hit me like a thunderbolt from heaven:

"I'd rather attempt to do something great and fail than attempt to do nothing and succeed."

- I went home, and the next Sunday in my pulpit I preached a sermon entitled "Courage to Make Your Dreams Come True." This gave the conspiratorial assistant pastor the motivation to move to stop me.
- The next day the newspaper carried a story of a school teacher in Minnesota who suddenly went insane and killed his wife and children. He was a pillar in his Lutheran church and in his community. The idea—demonic—came into my mind: *This could happen to you.* To me? To the nonviolent Schuller? Once and only once had I terminated a life. On my Iowa farm I shot a rabbit. I would never, ever pick up a gun again.

I tried to laugh my stress away.

I tried to pray it away.

I tried to talk it away.

But the fear would not go away. I could psychoanalyze it all right: I had shared my dream in public. Now there was an organized conspiracy to kill it. I had dared to face failure, but my subconscious was trying to tell me that if I failed I would be hurting myself, my wife, and my children. It would ruin all of us.

I cried out to God for help, but my prayers did not seem to heal me.

Then the night of the miracle. I went to bed as usual, praying with Arvella as I had every night since we were married. Again, I prayed passionately for help.

I awoke with a start in the middle of the night, overcome emotionally with a terrifying invasion of a demonic idea: "The hour you have feared is upon you. You are about to go over the brink." In what seemed just seconds, I was completely wet with the outpouring sweat of a cataclysmic horror.

I was lying flat on my back, arms extended, palms open, legs apart. Impulsively, I prayed a prayer that was part "Help!", part two-way:

**"Lord Jesus Christ. Are You dead or alive? I was taught to believe You are alive. If You are alive, can You hear me? Do You know what I'm going through? Do You care? Can You touch the core of my brain and remove this demonic fear that threatens to destroy me?"**

Then I was silent. I had done my part—laying my questions, my needs, my very soul before God. The next move was up to Him.

It wasn't long, only seconds, before I felt it. An invisible "finger" touched the top of my head. I could "feel" it pressing into my brain, like a finger poking deep into a bowl of mashed potatoes. I could feel it in there, as if it were three inches long. Then slowly God withdrew His "finger," taking with it the demonic ideas. A chill spread through my body, from the top of my head to the tips of my toes. Goose pimples erupted like a chorus to praise God for the miracle.

I was healed. The fear was gone. I had been touched by Jesus Christ. I knew it! I fell instantly into a deep, peaceful sleep.

## What Will Happen to My Dream?

The morning after the miracle, I awoke as daylight lit my window. Never before had I felt such transcendent, overwhelming peace! I was spiritually ecstatic! My soul had reached the mountaintop safely! My Guide had saved me from the precipice!

I recall leaving for work. Right outside our back door the roses were in bloom. The beauty thrilled me.

I went instantly back into the house and called to Arvella, "Honey, the roses are blooming this morning."

She called back, "Oh they've been blooming for the last two weeks."

I walked the short block to my office. The sun was shining. The clouds were white, gentle, and soft in the blue sky. I heard the birds singing.

I reached my office. The door was still locked. Where was my secretary? Some papers lay on the sidewalk by the door. I picked them up. The elder who had hired my assistant was now the vice president of the board. Here was a letter from him. He was resigning, it said. Another letter from the treasurer. He was resigning too.

I stepped inside. The telephone was ringing. It was my secretary. She wouldn't be coming in. She was quitting too. I couldn't blame her.

What would happen *now?* To my dream? To this church?

I stood alone—all alone in the center of my office. I looked up. I prayed. "I will build My church." The words consumed my consciousness. It was the voice of my Savior, who had touched and healed me only hours before. "*I* (not you but I) *will* (have no doubt—it is going to happen!) *build* (the dream will become a reality) *My church* (it will be *Mine*—you will give it up to Me; it will be *My* church—not Schuller's church)."

I stood, shocked, disenthroned but spiritually empowered! I extended my hand and pointed at my empty office chair and said, "Then, Lord, You take over! It's Yours. I'm tired. May I go on vacation?"

Betty Behr, a church member, offered us the use of her family's camping trailer, and we went on a two-week vacation in Sequoia National Park. I relaxed. I felt safe, secure, and serene.

Upon my return, I went to my office. The telephone rang. I picked it up. It was my assistant, the head of the conspiracy movement. "I'm calling to tell you I have just received a call to become the pastor of a vacant church in Norwalk," he said. "I'm leaving here."

The dark time was over. I sat down, and from my heart I penned a prayer.

Today, if there are flowers blooming and I do not see them, or birds singing and I do not hear them, clouds sliding silently through the soundless sea of space and I do not notice them, then come, Lord, to break through and touch me with Your miracle of mercy.

And I shall live the rest of my days in Your presence, power, and peace. Amen.

Two-way prayer. I asked. I waited. God answered. His dream of "a great church that hasn't been organized yet," His dream, entrusted to me, nurtured in prayer, was coming true. An amazing development in my soul's adventure with God.

ટ&

The next Sunday I preached this sermon:

## "The Five Phases of Faith"

1.  *The Nesting Phase*
    The nest is prepared. The egg is laid. The mind is expanded. The idea is deposited. A dream is born.
2.  *The Testing Phase*
    Questions are asked. Guidance is sought. Wisdom and courage are given—by God. You see the dream. You size it up. You seize it!
3.  *The Investing Phase*
    You make the announcement. You "go public" with the dream. You put your name and reputation on the line. And you "put your money where your mouth is."
4.  *The Arresting Phase*
    Opposition mounts. Negative forces move against you. You reach the point at which only God can make the dream happen. Hold on. Pray. Wait for His touch. You can and will succeed. The only way you can fail is if you give up.

5. *The Cresting Phase*
The mountain moves. The breakthrough happens. "And the time of the singing of birds has come" (Song 2:12, TLB). God crowns your faith with success.

Two-way prayer works wonders.

I knew that God was calling me to take a lifetime adventure with Him. He was giving me dreams, and He would help them to come true.

I was a young pastor. I made my share of mistakes. I needed God's guidance. He amply provided.

# Keeping Politics out of the Pulpit

When I was ordained, I was a political neophyte. Growing up, I never knew whether my parents were Democrat or Republican, and I couldn't care less. And I cannot recall ever coming under political influences or pressures in my four years of college and three years of seminary.

World War II raged. The Soviet Union and America were allies. By 1950 the war was over. I was ordained, and I stepped into the ministry. In 1955 I arrived in California politically neutral but quite possibly a liberal, at least in spirit.

I had not been in my new church long when I found the attendance growing. Having Norman Vincent Peale as a guest speaker had helped attract visitors. Two congressmen were in that crowd and would become members of my church. One was a Democrat, Clyde Doyle, and the other was a Republican, Jimmy Utt. I was in the middle. They both strongly advised me to keep politics out of the pulpit.

That was the precise advice I am sure God wanted to give me. Now, decades later, I can see that God wanted to make me a preacher who could bless all persons—Democrats and Republicans, conservatives and liberals, socialists and capitalists. But in the mid-fifties I had no understanding whatever of these "labels."

Fascists? I understood that. They were dictators. Communists? They were atheists. Both fascists and communists were "bad" and "dangerous," but I really didn't understand their platforms. I was inadequately informed.

In the late 1950s the anticommunist movement picked up press. I was introduced to it by the Democratic congressman Clyde Doyle. He'd been handpicked and appointed by President Roosevelt to sit on the House Un-American Activities Committee. Communism was only thirty-three years old as a world political movement when I was ordained. Marxism had been around longer. But communism was not discussed in my family, my denomination, or my training.

"Communism has become a global threat under Stalin," Congressman Doyle told me. "Stalin keeps a globe on his desk. His goal? To be history's first global emperor. He has spies in every country—including America."

Jimmy Utt agreed with Clyde Doyle. So anticommunism was something all Americans must agree on, I naively assumed. I should be informed, I was told. But the subject didn't interest me at all.

An Australian psychiatrist, Fred Schwartz, came to California to lecture on communism. I was given a free ticket and attended. The psychology of communism was intriguing. Dr. Schwartz was impressive. He came across as well educated and informed.

At the same time, Congressman Doyle told me that the government was terribly concerned about the communist conspiracy to take over and control the ports of Los Angeles and San Francisco. If Stalin planned a Pearl Harbor type attack, and we had just come through that not many years before, we had to be sure the "enemy" wouldn't come from the underground and control the seaports!

The twentieth century, I have since observed, was the "collectivist century." By that I mean a century that witnessed the popularization of shared, as opposed to individual, control over the production and distribution of goods. Collectivism started with Karl Marx, spawned socialism, and collided philosophically with individualism.

But in the fifties I would step into this confrontation of philosophies like a greenhorn. I had no inkling that many leaders in mainline Protestantism were sympathetic to Marxism as an alternative to capitalism, which they saw as systemically evil. Their thinking was, "Had not capitalism for centuries been driven by ruthless, often inhuman, exploitation of humanity, sacrificing laborers on the altar of money-making? Had not a capitalistic system produced child labor, slavery, wars, and depressions?"

This certainly was not what I had been taught in college or seminary. There were no anticapitalist teachings in my memory.

"Since 1945, communism has infiltrated over half the globe," I heard.

"All it needs to take over the world is for good people to do nothing," Dr. Schwartz warned. "Russia will hit us like Japan did, unless we are informed, knowledgeable, alert, and prepared to hold them back!"

I listened and remembered December 7, 1941. I didn't laugh. I became concerned.

Then the headlines of the nation's press suddenly focused on San Francisco. The House Committee on Un-American Activities was investigating communistic influences in the dockworkers union. Protestors appeared on the streets. Clyde Doyle, a member of that committee and a member of our church, a "liberal Democrat," was accused of being a fascist. That got my attention, for I knew that to be a lie!

"How do you handle the terrible things they're saying about you?" I asked him after a Sunday service.

"That's nothing," he said, "you should see what the Communists in Moscow say about us. I'll send you a copy of *Pravda*—the Communist paper in Russia. Just remember there are communists and pro-communists here in America today. Be alert. You'll find their viewpoints being promoted in all professions—college educators, entertainers, even theologians."

I had just heard an anticommunist lecturer warn about a corporate leader in America, Armand Hammer, whose father was one of the six founding members of the Communist Party in the United States. Armand had been an early and close friend of Lenin. The lecturer hinted that he was probably part of the Communist conspiracy in America. I had heard his name; I would never forget it.

Then two articles arrived in my mail. First, Clyde Doyle sent me the article from *Pravda* condemning his anticommunist activities. The Communist paper castigated in horrible sentences Clyde Doyle and their committee hearings in San Francisco.

That same week I received in the mail a pamphlet, sent to me by my denominational leader and printed by the National Council of the Churches of Christ, warning against the House Committee on Un-American Activities, which they called a terrible new fascist movement in America under the cloud of anticommunism.

I couldn't believe what this religious pamphlet said. The same sentences, the same paragraphs—identical to what I had just read in *Pravda!*

I was at the time one of the leading proponents of the National Council of the Churches of Christ. I loved their ecumenical, transdenominational spirit.

The pamphlet shattered my perceptions of the National Council of the Churches of Christ. I was sick. Were there communists, or at least *Pravda*-reading, *Pravda*-believing, pro-communists infiltrating the church?

Something inside of my sincere and youthful soul died—then and there.

I could not and would not allow my name and reputation to be linked to the National Council to which my denomination belonged. I saw in America a pro-communist movement gaining steam. I saw the birth of an anticommunist movement. Now I saw the emerging "anti-anticommunist" movement.

I felt betrayed by the ecumenical movement, which I now saw as an institution with its own political agenda.

I preached a sermon that made headlines in the daily newspaper in Garden Grove: "Schuller Blasts Judas in National Council."

I got bad mail from a Methodist pastor with the same name as mine, (spelled differently) Bob Shuler. "The name Ichabod will be carved over the door posts of your church," he wrote.

I was condemned by name in mainline Protestant church pulpits. I was "out" with the ministers who had been my friends. I felt alone, rejected, scorned, and abandoned.

I was now tempted for the first and last time to accept an invitation to go full-time into anticommunism and join Dr. Fred Schwartz. I could see America falling for communism the way many Germans, and even some Americans, including a young architect, Philip Johnson, were impressed by the work of Hitler not many years before.

I prayed deeply and passionately about what I should do.

The guidance I got from the Lord was clear: "Watch out for communism, and watch out for anticommunism, and watch out for anti-anticommunism."

I looked at the threat of communism and remembered what Lincoln said when he first saw a human being sold as a slave. "That's wrong. That's bad. When the time is right, I'll hit it and hit it hard."

For now I'd stay out of politics. I'd have to keep my focus on Jesus Christ and on human beings who were hurting and needing faith.

# What Is Your Deepest Need?

My soul's adventure with God continued. He was guiding, shaping, protecting, and preparing me. Here's how my faith and future would be shaped.

I cooled my overt, public "anticommunism." I could not and would not be drawn into confrontational political movements.

The preachers in America and around the world were in political war. I was out of it. "Avoid politics and you'll abdicate your prophetic role as a preacher," I was warned.

I couldn't agree. "I want to be a blessing to all persons," I argued. "I don't care what their politics are." But how could I do that? How could I safely and sensibly address the social injustices?

Guidance came through a fresh and new understanding of how best to communicate the gospel to unbelievers. I discovered the teaching of one of the leading psychiatrists of the time, Dr. Viktor Frankl.

"Sum it up for me, Dr. Frankl," I asked him after a lecture. "What is a human being's deepest need?" His answer would be pivotal in my soul's adventure.

"To Freud, the deepest need of the human is pleasure. I call it will to pleasure. Frustrate pleasure, and the human is in mental trouble.

"To Adler, the deepest need is power. The will to power is the central core of the human personality.

"To me, they're not on target. To me it's the will to meaning. The human soul must not, cannot, be stripped of its will to meaning."

He definitely had my attention. "Why is *meaning* so all important?" I asked.

He looked at me, puzzled and perplexed. "I don't know why meaning is our deepest need—I just know that it is."

I would continue to probe, study, read about, and analyze that question about our deepest need.

I attended a psychiatric conference in Madrid, Spain. The year was 1967. More than four thousand psychiatrists from around the world—including Communists from the Soviet Union—were present. I was one of a few theologians in attendance.

The program listed the final morning lectures under the title "Human Values in Psychotherapy." The first lecturer's topic was "*Faith*—A Human Value in Psychotherapy."

"Man needs to have faith in something," he said. "Even if you're an unbeliever, don't ridicule the faith of your patients. Respect their faith. Find something positive in it and build on it to create a healing therapy."

I was impressed.

The second lecturer was from Germany. His topic: "*Hope*—A Human Value in Psychotherapy."

"Hope," he said, "is a human phenomenon none of us can explain. But we all have seen its healing and transforming power when it comes into a sick patient."

*Is this a secular convention? It's almost religious,* I began to think.

The third lecturer, from Peru, spoke on "Love—A Human Value in Psychotherapy."

"The most healing power that can come into a personality is love, nonjudgmental love," he said. My heart leaped! "And we psychiatrists are the only people who can help guilt-ridden souls," he went on. "For we have a neutral position on morality and are free from the temptations to impose our values on persons. So we can truly forgive, because we have not been offended," he declared.

*Wait a minute!* I thought to myself. *You're wrong! Only the offended can forgive!* And in my mind's eye I saw the cross of Christ. When an amoral or immoral person "forgives," it lacks power and integrity. But when an innocent person has been wrongly accused and he chooses to forgive, then pardon has integrity and power!

I went home, prepared to preach passionately the gospel of Christ, the only religious message that called people to live out "faith, hope, and love, and the greatest of these is love."

I was being prepared to become more of a blessing to people!

The third key event in the shaping of my faith and future again involved Dr. Frankl. A meeting was scheduled for the two of us— alone, for three hours!—in my office on the twelfth floor of the church in Garden Grove, California. It was 1969.

"Have you found the answer to the question 'Why is meaning the deepest desire in the human heart?' " I asked.

"No, I have not," he answered.

"I believe I have!" I said. He looked surprised. He listened respect-fully.

"It's human dignity, Dr. Frankl. I found it in the Bible. In the book of Psalms it is written, 'And God crowned man with glory and honor,' " I said.

"Dr. Frankl, life has meaning only when and if it preserves the one thing no person can live healthfully without—*dignity* as a human being. I cannot, must not, will not survive if I am stripped of all glory, honor, dignity, and self-respect.

"Dignity, self-love, self-esteem, self-worth—that's the ultimate human emotional hunger!"

I preached! Yes, I preached it!

I had found the positive preacher's building block. Regardless of race, religion, politics, culture, economics, or theology, I'd found the spiritual key—I was sure of it!

I wrote my most important book, *Self-Love: The Dynamic Force of Success.* The year was 1969. In the years that followed, I synergized

the psychology of self-love with positive Calvinistic theology and published the book *Self-Esteem: The New Reformation.*

Twenty-five years later, I visited Dr. Frankl in his private home in
Vienna to thank him for being one of the most helpful, enlightening,
and inspiring professors to shape my soul.

God was shaping my soul to preach His blessed gospel to the
whole world. Believers and unbelievers would listen.

## Here's How Two-Way Prayer Works

We needed property, at least ten acres, to build the church I had
described to Dr. Peale. I looked for land, and off a back street in
Garden Grove I found it. Ten acres of beautiful orange trees. What a
place of peace. We could build there and move out of the drive-in
theater.

I made a Monday morning appointment with the owner. "She's
a widow and wanting to sell," I had been told. The Sunday afternoon
before the appointment, I walked into that grove alone. I opened my
Bible and read the words of Jesus. "Whatever you ask for in prayer,
believe that you have received it, and it will be yours" (Mark 11:24
NIV). I knelt down and prayed and claimed that promise. I was ready
for tomorrow morning. This would be the perfect location for my
"George Truett Church."

The next morning my realtor put the papers before the owner.
He had made all the arrangements. I was there only to witness the
owner's signature and sign myself.

She reached for the ballpoint pen. It didn't work. She scratched
it on another piece of paper and saw the black ink ooze out. She raised
the instrument and lowered it to the line. Then stopped. She looked
up, as if she was looking for someone.

"I really don't know," she said. "I'm not sure my husband would
agree if he were still here. He just loved this orange grove." Tears
formed, and she began to cry. She laid the pen down. "I'm sorry. I'm
so sorry."

My faith took a tailspin. "Jesus, You promised!" I declared later, alone with Him in two-way prayer.

"I've got a better idea." The words rushed into my mind.

One week later the realtor called. "I've found another piece. It's ten acres."

"Tell me more. Where is it and what's the cost?" I asked.

"Good news, bad news," he answered. "The good news is the price is only half what we were going to pay the widow—sixty-six thousand dollars. Eighteen thousand down, and the owner will carry the mortgage at 6 percent interest. That's four hundred dollars a month for fifteen years."

"The bad news?"

"It's not downtown in Garden Grove. It's way out on the outskirts. That's why it's cheap."

We had only three thousand dollars in all of our church accounts. We opened an escrow. We would have 120 days to raise the $18,000 down payment. No sooner had we agreed to buy it when the big news broke. The state unveiled plans to extend the biggest freeway ever built in California, and it would run right by this property! The church would be in downtown Orange County! The location was much better than the orange grove! Suddenly the owner hoped we would fail—he was selling too cheap. We struggled, begged, and borrowed in a fund-raising drive and made the down payment only three hours before the 120-day escrow was to terminate!

I got the message! *See, Bob. I answered the prayer of your heart—not of your lips. This is a better place.*

"But how can we afford the monthly payment of four hundred dollars?" the church treasurer asked me. I didn't know.

The very next Sunday, a check for one hundred dollars was in the offering plate. Again the next week. Again the next and the next week. The donors, strangers to us at the time, did not have an inkling of our need. Their names: Vernon and Lavon Dragt. It was their weekly tithe! Their monthly tithe matched perfectly the monthly payment on our new land mortgage.

Years later, the same donors would make a generous leadoff gift to help build the Tower of Hope, which would house the nation's first twenty-four-hour, live, suicide-prevention telephone counseling service, manned by hundreds of volunteers. Now, after more than twenty-five years, it's the longest-running crisis telephone ministry in a church in the United States.

Two-way prayer. You ask, you listen; God speaks and acts. A connection! Here, faith crests with all glory to God and honor to His people of faith.

# I'M QUIET—
# AND I'M
# LISTENING

*Relax, Retreat, Receive, Resign, Recharge, and Renew.*

"BE STILL, AND KNOW THAT I AM GOD."
— PSALM 46:10 —

# Chapter 9

# The Heavens Are Opening Up to Me!

I'm losing you! Can you hear me? I can't hear you."

"I think I'm out of range."

"I've got a lot of static on my end."

Everyone with a cellular telephone has made these statements at one time or another!

If you can't tune in, how can you turn on?

Are the lines overloaded? Is a hill or a mountain or a high-rise building cutting out the sharp clear signal?

Don't throw the phone away. Make the move that gets you clearly back on line.

Stress produces static in the spirit!

It's time to shift your prayer to another channel. Call it—meditation.

Meditation—it's getting prayer back on a direct line.

Meditation is withdrawing from the distractions of the world that would disrupt the messages that God is sending you.

Meditation is quietly, honestly, sincerely setting aside the pressures of culture, ego, purse, property, or pride.

Meditation. The Bible teaches it. Saints through the ages have practiced it. It's a distinctive, refreshing level of prayer.

In meditation, under the watchful care of God's Holy Spirit, we open ourselves to a cleaner and clearer communication channel of prayer.

Meditation? Here I open my eyes, my ears, my mind, and my heart to God: "I'm open. I'm listening, God. I can hear You now."

Meditation—it's really a wonder-working prayer channel.

Some years ago on my soul's adventure with God, I began to picture my brain as a car with a sunroof, open to heaven's light. I'm always thinking, *listening* (yes, that's praying), whether I'm visiting with family, presiding over meetings, or doing seemingly mundane tasks around the office or house.

"Be . . . continuing steadfastly in prayer," St. Paul teaches (Rom 12:10, 12). To me, this means, "Keep connected to God at all times." I relate this to all the Bible promises in which God tells me: "I am with you always" (Matt. 28:20), and "I will never leave you nor forsake you" (Heb. 13:5).

See your mind as a sunroof. Stay on the edge of being "connected" to God. God is alive, transcending space, time, and boundaries—intellectual boundaries, relationship boundaries, emotional boundaries, theological boundaries. Through meditation the mind is opened to divinely instigated spiritual management, which releases the power of Possibility Thinking.

Meditation—call it "soul searching" or "heart searching" until a simple secret source of spiritual blockage is discovered.

Meditation has been, for my soul, an emotional and spiritual therapy for managing my mental activity, my memories, my moods, and my motives.

Do you sometimes feel as though your communication channel to God is blocked? You cannot feel His presence or the flow of His power? You're "disconnected"? You don't know why?

One time the air-conditioning system went out in our church. Maintenance engineers checked meters and systems and could find nothing wrong. The experts were dumbfounded until a painter discovered a dead insect in the thermostat on the wall. It had cut off the connection!

One of my dearest church members is the celebrity pianist Roger Williams. He had perfect pitch, but health problems hit him and his gift was suddenly gone. Someone suggested that he see my friend, the world-famous Dr. Howard House, founder of the House Ear Institute in Los Angeles. Here the shocking discovery was made: A tiny fleck of hair had dropped into Roger's ear canal when he had been to the barber. It was removed, and his hearing was restored!

Out of touch? Is there static in your prayer life? Try shifting prayer to the level called meditation. You may be surprised to discover some stress, conflict, tension, or sin that is cutting off your connection with Christ.

## Overwhelmed? Then Meditate!

Have trouble remembering names? Where you placed the keys? What you were going to say?

Why do you have problems with your memory? It's overload. Mental overload.

Our fast, noisy, tension-generating culture can choke and clog the clear and open channel with the Eternal Spirit!

Humans were spiritually and emotionally engineered to talk, to listen, to communicate with one another on a one-to-one relationship with a look, a word, and a touch. That is biological reality!

Two persons—call them Adam and Eve—they're in the garden. Connecting, communicating, creating.

Hold on. Fast forward from the Garden of Eden to the twentieth century. Now there's a car. No, two cars. A house. More keys. A telephone. An answering machine. A pager. A fax machine. A television set. A radio. A CD player. Add a computer. Don't forget a cellular phone—it's got to go with you everywhere. In the car. In the garden (ouch!). To lunch in the restaurant. Oh, yes. The newspaper. Stop at the mailbox. Junk mail. Another letter from whom? Where did they get my address?

We will meet a *lot* of new people today. We will be introduced by phone, fax, computer, television, radio, cellular phone, and Internet! By paper mail and E-mail! "My gosh, what was that guy's name again?

I forget. When and where did I meet him? I can't remember. I must be getting older."

Of course you are.

You're also overloaded! You're overwhelmed! You're out of touch! *You need meditation.*

So learn now how to switch channels and make a clear and clean connection with the Holy Spirit! "In quietness and confidence will be your strength." Hear God's wise words once more. "Be still and know that I am God."

Try meditation. Here's how:

1. *Relax.* **Get the body—with its demands, its desires, its distractions—*out of the way!***
2. *Retreat.* **Leave behind your tensions, stress, and passions. Put your anxieties in neutral. Give God a chance to refresh your spirit and revitalize your soul.**
3. *Receive.* **Welcome the Spirit of the Lord. God's Spirit is within you. Experience the presence, the peace, and the power of the living God again! Open your mind. Let the sacred stillness subdue the stress that can block the creative flow of God's Spirit within you.**
4. *Resign.* **Emotionally surrender your ambitions for a moment. Mentally tell yourself, "I am retired. I'm free at last!"**
5. *Recharge.* **Fill your thoughts to overflowing with the truth found in Scripture and the Creator's work you see and sense around you.**
6. *Renew!* **Pick up the strong spiritual signals God is sending out to you. Hear a fresh divine call to a new adventure. Catch the rush of new opportunities. You'll soon come back out of retirement! Prayer power is turned back on again!**

Meditation must become a part of the unfolding prayer process of the nutritionally fit soul, just like preparation and cultivation of the soil must precede the seed time and harvest.

As I mentioned earlier, praying, in many ways, is like farming.

- In the first step, the soil must be broken, disked, and raked until it is prepared to receive the seed. In prayer, your soul must first be prepared by faith.
- Then the seed must be dropped. In Level Two prayer, your call for help must be raised.
- Then the weeds must be removed. In prayer, the negative elements in your thoughts and feelings must be eliminated like static on the line. You clear the channel and reprogram your mind with positive ideas and moods.
- And water must be supplied. In prayer, renewed vision, purpose, and enthusiasm must be added to your soul.

I have found that if I do not allow my soul to be freshened and revitalized in this way, through periods of quiet, respectful meditation with God, my life soon resembles the cracked, crusty surface of a field that has gone several seasons without rain.

Shh! Quiet. Be still. Whisper. "Hear" God's Spirit speak to your inner ear. Relax and let God reshape your soul. Reach out. Welcome His stroking that soothes your stress.

Now you are surrendered to His Holy Spirit. Now you are worshiping God! Enjoy these moments! Here miracles will happen! Be renewed!

Move into mighty moods of meditation. Draw energy from centers of sacred solitude, serenity, and silence. Jesus advised this! "When you pray, go into your room, and when you have shut your door, pray to your Father who is in the secret place; and your Father who sees in secret will reward you openly" (Matt. 6:6). Find yourself coming alive in the garden of prayer called *meditation.*

## Creativity through Tranquility

Yes, the Bible teaches meditation. The human mind and soul were designed and engineered to receive spiritual signals sent from the eternal God to your sensitive and seeking soul.

I learned much about this powerful principle through one of the truly great architects of the twentieth century, Richard Neutra.

Once our church property was in hand, we needed an extremely talented architect to design a creative, new worship facility. I envisioned an innovative design that would bring together in one garden setting a "drive-in" church and a "walk-in" congregation.

Richard Neutra's face had just appeared on the cover of *Time* magazine. He was in touch with Renee DuBos, the founder of sociobiology, who advanced the idea that every living organism has its own natural habitat.

"Ruin the natural environment," DuBos observed, "and you'll take the living organism out of its natural, healthy habitat. It will desperately accept deviations in its life-or-death struggle to survive. It will become a deviate before it surrenders to extermination."

Neutra learned from DuBos the need to know and respect every biological organism's distinctive demand for its natural, healthy environment. This, then, must dictate any architectural design.

To Neutra, that raised a question: What is the human being? What is his primal nature? What environment will nurture his natural, healthy state of being?

I met Richard Neutra. We agreed the human being was designed to be a creative communicator. For that reason, humans were placed in an environment that induced creativity—God put Adam and Eve in a garden! Creativity takes place in a space and state where communication can flow freely.

The conscious and subconscious mind must be tranquil and tension-free to communicate with God. So the natural habitat for the human was a garden.

In the garden the human could be relaxed and receptive. Here he could "meditate"—think creatively. So the human was given eyes, ears, and skin to sense and respond to stress-reducing stimuli. These spiritual stimuli channel tranquility into the brain to relax the creative centers of human consciousness. Creativity through tranquility!

To be normal, healthy, creative human beings, we must have the opportunity to be in a natural space in which sounds, sights, and smells relax us and make us receptive to creative ideas, impulses, and moods. But take us out of the garden and our spirits will become distorted. Creativity will be stifled or stunned or turned into a deviate force by stresses, strains, sounds, and sights that cause spiritual static, which interferes with God's silent signals being sent to us.

"Architecture must be biologically realistic," Neutra taught.

*Architecture must provide an environment that prepares the mind, body, and soul for an intimate encounter with God's Spirit,* I thought. I became a convert to Neutra's philosophy of architecture, biorealism.

# Preaching to the Architects

Years after meeting Neutra, I was elected member of the board of directors of the American Institute of Architecture. I was invited to give the opening speech to five thousand architects at their national convention in St. Louis, Missouri. There was understandable criticism when the board invited a preacher to bring the keynote address. I was received with mild but polite applause.

"How many of you, in your architectural education, were exposed to biorealism?" was my opening sentence. Only a few hands went up.

"Then permit me to say a few words."

"The human being is not living in his natural habitat," I began. "The eyes do not look on trees bending in the breeze or on white clouds in blue skies. We are missing the meditative experience of a full moon bathing grass, water, and flowers in the garden. Instead the eye looks on electric power poles, cracked cement, asphalt streets with potholes.

"The ear does not hear the trickle of water dripping from branches or tumbling tranquilly in the brook, the whisper of the breeze, the music of falling leaves, the singing of the birds. All of these are drowned out by unnatural and tension-generating noise: the roar of engines, the shifting of gears, the wail of sirens, the moan of racing ambulances. The sensory elements of humanity are now sending stress-generating signals to the subconscious.

"The human organism was designed to be a powerful, creative, healthy, communicator when left in its natural habitat. Take the human biological organism out of its normal habitat and the human body will generate stress instead of serenity. Stress will sever the spirit of creative communication.

"The human being will become a deviate in his desperation to survive in a dangerous, destructive habitat. The spirit will be stifled by the static of stress.

"Which explains why secularism and cynicism have replaced natural, normal, and healthy spiritual creativity. Clear spiritual signals from God are lost. Emotional static cuts off the connection between God and humans, the way a cellular phone loses contact when it is moved out of range of the satellite or tower that sends the messages.

"The result? Look around you. Atheism flourishes in the noisy cities. Spiritual life comes naturally in the stillness of the garden, moonlight, and meadow.

"The atheist's spiritual insensitivity is a deviation from the natural human norm. The atheist is a deviate!

"Take the human out of the garden and he'll be out of touch.

"Create architecture that blocks out the tension-generating noise and the sights of tension-generating views. Create architecture to maximize tranquility. Make it possible to meditate and be healthfully creative."

I finished the forty-five minute lecture, and never before or since was I more proud and pleased to receive a rousing standing ovation. Thank You, Lord.

৵

Meditation. It's basic. You go emotionally back to your garden—your natural habitat. You will become a truly *human* being, a whole and healthy person.

Meditation kept me sane and healthy during my most difficult times. I could not have maintained spiritual health if I had not remained open and well connected with God.

The radio, television, and telephone were all part of an environment that set me up to receive messages likely to generate tension. I discovered that I could only be creative when I was protected from any possibility of uninvited, pressure-producing interruptions.

I went to the garden. It became my healing hobby. There among my roses, their buds just opening to greet the morning sun, I found the peace of God. I was where God put Adam. Here, I was back in my natural habitat.

## Reacquainted with the Creator

One of my dearest friends during the years we built our church was a woman I called "the First Lady of Orange County"—Athalie Irvine Clark. The largest landowner in Orange County was the Irvine Company. James Irvine, Sr., was the founder. His son married Athalie, who would become the grande dame of the highest social set in Southern California—from Beverly Hills to Palm Springs to Newport Beach.

When I hired Richard Neutra to design our first buildings, Athalie took notice. When the first Neutra structures rose, she drove by. When we erected the fourteen-story office tower to house the twenty-four-hour telephone counseling center (also to house a professional counseling center with psychologists and theologians working together), Athalie was attracted.

She came to visit me. We became close friends. In her life she had known closely, intimately, the power people of her day. From Albert Einstein to Richard Nixon to John Wayne. And now she opened her heart and soul and purse to this ministry that bridged science and religion—merging the sacred with the secular. Here she discovered that real truths will never collide—they will always coincide.

Athalie understood the absolute need for humans to be close to their Creator. Later, she served as a director on my ministry board and donated her historic forty-acre estate in Maui, Hawaii, to become a retreat, where people could rest and relax away from the pressures of our noisy world.

At her invitation I became a part-time resident of the Hawaiian Islands. We held retreats for ministers on the Maui ranch, where we designed some "meditation spots" to take advantage of the lush, tropical beauty.

I carefully placed benches alongside a gently falling stream. I placed them so the eye could only see trees, sky, flowers, and waterfalls. No streets. No cars. No telephone poles. No rooftops. The ear could hear only the sacred stillness of the serene garden. A rustle. A bird's song. A palm frond swishing slowly in a tender breeze. The gentle sound of a bubbling brook.

Here our guests were asked to sit—alone, eyes and ears open—and meditate on the questions that would reacquaint them with creation and draw them to the Creator:

1. **What do I see?**

   **Mountain peaks in the distance? A hummingbird on the red ginger? A leaf taking a happy trip down the little stream?**

   **Mentally list all the flowers you can see. The spectrum of color. What else? Pebbles? Plants? Little fish in the crystal clear brook? Ants busy at work? Don't miss a thing. God created it all. Everything has a purpose. See it! Really see it! See it all change before your eyes. Notice the sun is suddenly shining where a moment ago there were shadows. It's time for a plant to draw its energy from a few precious moments of direct sunlight.**

   **Ready? Have you seen everything? Then move on to question two.**

2. **What do I hear?**

   **Listen. Come alive. Wake up. It's a new day! Nature is all around you, breathing, living, making sounds. Water. Wind. Birds flying and walking and running.**

   **What's that, far in the distance? You noticed it for only a second or two. The sound must have been an airplane. It came. It did not know you were here. It need not distract you.**

You are alone with creation. You are near to the Creator here and now. This is your real world. This is your natural habitat. Your soul is at home here.

3. *What do I feel?*

Pray this simple prayer:

> *Oh God—what do I see?*
> *What do I feel?*
> *Now help me to know what in life is real.*

Relax until you cannot feel one part of your body pressing against another. Shoes—remove them. Belts—loosen them until you cannot feel them. Yes, uncross your legs.

Relax all parts of your body. Reach out spiritually. Receive the Spirit of God who is here. Thank Him! You are close to God in His garden.

A sign in the garden at my home bears an old poem:

> *The kiss of the sun for pardon.*
> *The song of the bird for mirth.*
> *One is nearer God's heart in a garden*
> *Than anywhere else on earth.*

Yes, many a time my soul would have been thrown into overload if I had not learned to run away with God and get alone with Him in the garden!

Meditation works miracles!

# The Uninvited Touch of God

If you invite even the hardest atheist to experience fully the garden, he will encounter God. God's creation, if we will allow it, will speak quietly—and effectively.

"The heavens declare the glory of God." The psalmist David, experiencing this connection in Psalm 19:1, tells it better than I. No matter who you are, what your faith, or even if you declare no faith at all, in a moment of beauty it is very possible that you will experience the uninvited touch of God in your life.

I observed this amazing experience with the famous architect Philip Johnson. He has, on more than one occasion, told people he is an atheist. I knew that as I worked with him through the years. He had the freedom to make that choice. I never quarreled with him about it.

The last assignment that we gave him was the designing of the bell tower of the Crystal Cathedral. It would be 236 feet high. It needed to appear to be all glass to harmonize with the Cathedral. It must house a complete carillon—a set of fifty-two bronze bells. The engineering would be a challenge.

Philip came up with a design that was stunning. He showed the tower, completely faced with faceted slabs of number-nine stainless steel that would sparkle like icicles, reflecting flowers, trees, and light.

The design was constructed.

Philip was to see the tower for the first time on the morning when it would be dedicated in a great event of celebration. He arrived in town the night before. We had him picked up before sunrise, for I wanted a chance to be alone with him. I wanted to walk with him through the gardens on the cathedral campus and watch the morning light reflect off the diamond-shaped tips of the sculptured twenty-three-story mirrored tower.

We greeted each other in the cathedral gardens. Then we looked up. The tower sparkled like a million diamonds. Philip was spiritually shocked!

"Come, Philip. We have to walk around the thirty acres to see it from every angle," I said.

As we strolled, the tower changed before our very eyes. It picked up the hues of the morning sunrise. Pink. Blue. Faceted edges of the stainless steel suddenly caught the first rays of the rising sun and reflected them into our eyes! We could not speak. We were awestruck.

It was an amazing spiritual experience.

Philip stopped. He looked at me, and his usually cool eyes became misty. Then I saw it. His lips trembled. They actually quivered!

"Bob," he said, "this morning I will confess to my sin of arrogance. I thought I knew all about materials. I thought I knew all about design. I thought I knew how light could interact and interplay in the creative process with glass, stainless steel, and water." He paused. His lips were still trembling. He confessed: "*Somebody* was helping me with this design."

I thanked God, then and there.

Later that morning, Philip would stand in the pulpit of the Crystal Cathedral, looking at a packed house, and speak to the television cameras that would take his message to millions of people around the world: "This morning I confess to the sin of arrogance." He repeated what he had spoken to me privately. "Someone beyond me helped design this Crystal Cathedral bell tower!"

In Franz Schulze's biography of Philip Johnson, Schulze mentions that a reporter who had known Philip for many years was shocked at hearing him speak so sincerely, so spiritually. Later, the reporter asked, "Philip, how could you say that?"

Philip replied, "Yes. Wasn't that awful!"

It was quite easy for him to deny the integrity of what probably was the greatest encounter he had ever had with the God of creation! Out of sight of the sparkling experience, surrounded again by people and objects and foreign sounds and sights, it was quite easy for him to fall back into a state of emotional and spiritual deviation.

# Chapter 10

# Overwhelmed? Overloaded? Here's Relief!

Yes, the "New Agers" have grabbed hold of meditation. Eccentric religionists and far-out psychological therapies have taken off with it.

A stewardess on a plane came to serve me. As she leaned forward to place my coffee, her necklace swung close to my face. Attached to the gold chain was a beautiful sculptured prismatic crystal. It sparkled. I reached toward it.

Startled and alarmed, she withdrew quickly and said, almost angrily, "Don't touch it. Salt from your fingers will block the spiritual energy it radiates."

I apologized. I raised my eyebrows. *This is the late twentieth century, and intelligent people fall for this superstition?* I asked myself.

The reality is that in today's world, mental overload presses our biological limits. The eyes cannot absorb all that they see; the ears cannot listen to all that they hear. The brain can process only so much data at a time. Overload demands relief.

Hey, Christian! Hear me! Let's not give up the glorious God-given gift of meditation by turning it over to those outside our faith! Meditation not only offers the opportunity for spiritual rejuvenation, it can help make our stressful, overloaded lives more peaceful and productive.

But just how do you meditate?

Surprise! You may already be enjoying simple meditation and not realize it! People often think that meditation only happens if and when they sit cross-legged with all ten fingers touching, eyes fixed in a self-hypnotic trance.

Positive meditation is creative thinking. Attend church regularly. There you will find release and retreat from worldly distractions! The subconscious knows that it is safe there and will not be exposed to tension-generating interruptions.

In church you can experience seclusion, security, serenity. And yes, honestly, you will recall your mistakes. Here in the sacred sanctuary your sins can be forgiven. This is redemptive meditation.

Look up. See the cross. Your sins can be pardoned. "Forgive me, Lord," your soul whispers to Jesus. Peace!

You are renewed! Like a car after a wash job! Clean. New. Sparkling.

Now you are open and receptive to God's communication. An idea comes into your mind. Maybe from the music. Maybe from the sermon. Occasionally from out of the blue. A solution to a problem! Yes!

Meditation works miracles in the mind.

Of course, God touches us where we live and work when we pray and connect with Him and allow His Spirit to connect with our spirit. That's constructive, creative, positive meditation.

Meditation. Yes, it is as "elementary" as going to church.

ॐ

Arvella and I arrived in California in February of 1955. Two weeks later I had found the drive-in theater where I would start holding services. I announced my plans by putting an ad in the newspaper and by distributing flyers door to door: "Starting Sunday, March 27, a new church will hold services at 11:00 A.M. in the Orange Drive-In Theater. Come as you are in the family car."

The organ I'd bought en route to California arrived. I bought a used two-wheel trailer and put the organ on it. I would pull it behind my car.

I met two men, Theo Weaver and Dean DeVries, in the neighborhood coffee shop. We got to talking, and I told them who I was, what I was going to do. They laughed. They agreed to help me out, to "usher" at the drive-in theater and take up the offering.

I was getting excited!

On Saturday, March 20, eight days before our opening church service, the doorbell rang. It was an ultraconservative minister from my denomination.

"You mean you're going to start a church in the drive-in theater? That's terrible! That's not a place to go and worship God," he said.

When he left, I was a scared twenty-eight-year-old boy. Was he right? Was I making a big mistake? I had prayed; I felt sure I was guided by God. Now this pastor had injected me with self-doubt.

Suddenly my enthusiasm disappeared. My excitement was gone. My self-confidence was shattered. I didn't believe in me anymore. It was now Saturday night, March 19. A week from tomorrow, Sunday, March 27, would be opening day for our new church. Should I go through with it?

Everything was arranged. I had spent all my money (five hundred dollars) on advertisements, a pulpit, a cross and altar I'd built myself, a two-wheel trailer to pull the organ, and a microphone. If I quit now, I would walk away from the money my denomination entrusted to me—all spent and wasted.

The next morning, Sunday, March 20. I was scared. "Honey, let's go to Hollywood Presbyterian Church this morning," I said to Arvella. "I'd like to hear Dr. Raymond Lindquist preach."

We made the one-hour drive to Hollywood and found seats in the middle of a packed church.

I prayed quietly. I *relaxed*. I *retreated*. I *renewed* my spirit. I *repented*. "Lord, forgive me if I made a mistake." I *received*. Yes, meditation was doing something to me! Miraculously!

Dr. Lindquist stepped into his pulpit, not knowing I was there; where I had come from; how I had seen the deer from my train window; how I had found a drive-in theater; how one of the denominational pastors had called on me only yesterday to admonish, chastise, and correct me; how I was "coming apart" inside.

My soul was scared. The dream was under attack. I needed help for the journey!

"The title of my message today," Dr. Lindquist said, "is printed on your morning's program."

I looked at the program: "God's Formula for Your Self-Confidence!" Wow! Just what I needed. The Scripture printed underneath would engrave itself forever in my memory, my mind, my heart, my spirit, my brain, my soul.

> BEING CONFIDENT OF THIS VERY THING, THAT HE WHO HAS BEGUN A
> GOOD WORK IN YOU WILL COMPLETE IT. (PHIL. 1:6)

I would meditate on these words the rest of my life!

I would never forget Dr. Lindquist's words: "Build your self-confidence. You need it. You're lost without it. You must have a powerful and strong self-confidence.

"But build it: *Not on might*. 'I can do it all by myself.' No.

"*Not on magic*. Forget superstition, whether it's in religion, astrology, or occult teachings. Use your head. Be intelligent.

"*Build it on the mercy of God*. He got you where you are today. He has started you on your way. God will never quit what He starts!"

I became impassioned! Empowered! A super Possibility Thinker!

I walked out of church, remembering my first prayer only a little more than twenty years before—"Make me a preacher when I grow up." *My confidence was renewed.*

God started me in my ministry. God gave me that vision through my uncle. Being a preacher wasn't my idea!

And God brought me here to California. And He lined up a drive-in theater for the first service of our new church. Here we would be close to the sky, the sun, the trees, the birds! Here I would be close to nature. God knew that before I was aware of biorealism.

Now, through the Bible, in that hour of meditation, God gave me a gift that would keep my soul strong for the whole adventure: "Being confident of this very thing, that He who has begun a good work in you will complete it" (Phil. 1:6).

The mercy of God. He loves me. He cares about me. He has faith in me! I would not fail. The following Sunday a great church would be born!

I got it—super self-confidence balanced with true humility—through meditation and a soul-strengthening sentence from Scripture.

When your pride is rooted in the gifts and grace of God, your humility will be assured! "It is *God* who works in you to will and to act according to His good purpose" (Phil. 2:13, italics added). My insecurity vanished. I was moving ahead with mountain-moving meditation!

Meditation! In church! What a powerful place to begin a new ministry.

I had been reminded that I had something inside me that transcended a personal philosophy of Possibility Thinking. I had faith in the power and presence of God. I was not in this alone. My soul was once again ready to press on with the adventure—with God.

## Be Careful What You Pray For!

For nearly six years, the drive-in theater was my church. But now the time had come for a permanent walk-in, drive-in church. Our first church was built, but it soon became too small for the growing congregation. A master plan was developed, culminating in what is now the world-renowned Crystal Cathedral. Green "pastures," still waters, trees, and flowers were designed in that master plan.

"Dr. Schuller, there is a beautiful, larger-than-life-size bronze statue of Jesus feeding His sheep that you should see," an acquaintance said excitedly. "The sculptor is from Munich, Germany. He escaped Hitler and came to California, where he's been working. This piece of art would be beautiful in the church gardens."

"I'm sorry," I replied. "I'm not interested in sculpture. It's not something that interests me." I had never learned to appreciate sculpture as a child or a young man.

"Think about it. Pray about it. Check it out," he urged. "Remember his name: Henry Van Wolf. His studio is on Van Nuys Boulevard. If you're ever there, you can't miss it. It's a little barn just off the freeway."

I heard what he said, but I wasn't a bit interested.

Many months passed. Just as I was preparing to leave one morning to study at the Fuller Seminary library, I noticed a copy of a prayer someone had sent me. It was written by Norman Grubb. I really liked it, so I carried it in my hand to my car, thinking I could memorize it while I was making the long drive on the freeway.

Before I started the car I read it aloud.

*Good morning, Lord!*
*What are You up to today?*
*Can I be a part of it?*
*Thank You. Amen.*

In the quiet solitude of my car, I was protected from any possibility of uninvited, pressure-producing interruptions—this solitude was the perfect mental climate for meditation.

I drove away from our home. A streetlight turned red. I read the prayer again.

On the freeway, I repeated the prayer, over and over again. Oops! I missed my exit! I should have been paying attention to the road instead of absentmindedly memorizing the prayer. I had no idea where the next exits would take me.

Then right in front of me I saw the huge green sign: "Van Nuys Blvd. Exit." Van Nuys Boulevard? I remembered the sculptor's studio. Why not?

Impulsively, I exited the freeway, and there was the barn. I pulled into the little parking lot, got out, and knocked on the door.

An elderly man, white-haired, dressed in the classic sculptor's white smock opened the door. "Yes?" he said in a thick German accent. "Come in."

There in the high-ceilinged studio were scattered bronze pieces.

Dominating the room was the larger-than-life-size bronze sculpture of the shepherd and the sheep. To my surprise, I was impressed! The shepherd's right hand looked strong holding his staff. His face radiated gentleness. His left hand was feeding a mother sheep. A lamb was in the position to nurse from the mother. The piece was really, really beautiful.

*Strong but tender!* I thought. *That's my Lord.*

"Dr. Schuller," the sculptor said, "I'm so depressed. I need money. I have to sell it. It's been finished for years now, and only earlier this morning I believe I may have found a buyer. Kay Gable was here and may buy it for the front entrance of her Episcopal church, as a memorial to her husband, the actor Clark Gable."

"But Mr. Van Wolf, I know that church. The front door is off a sidewalk by a street where buses and cars ride by. It's dirty and noisy. This piece belongs in green pastures beside still waters!" Without thinking, these words tumbled out of my mouth. "This belongs in the garden of my church! How much will it cost to buy it?"

"I told Mrs. Gable I wanted twenty-five thousand dollars. But if you have such a place, I'd sell it to you for twenty-two thousand. But I need to sell it today. She's coming back tomorrow for another look."

We discussed the price. The terms. All I had to my name was six hundred dollars in a hospital savings account to cover the cost of the baby my wife would deliver in six weeks.

"Could you accept a down payment of six hundred dollars, with the balance to be paid in twenty-four monthly payments?" What was I saying?

He agreed.

I got a blank sheet of paper from my briefcase and wrote out a purchase contract. Six hundred dollars down, twenty-four monthly payments of one thousand dollars a month—interest and principal. I signed it. He signed it. I wrote out a check for six hundred dollars.

"I'll have to switch the money from a savings account to my checking account," I explained. "I'll do that this afternoon."

He smiled. It was an answer to prayer as far as he was concerned.

He would come out tomorrow to check the location and make plans to deliver and install it.

I was jubilant! Over sculpture? Me? I shook my head in disbelief over what I had done.

One week later the sculpture was at its new home in the church gardens. Beautiful! Inspiring! I was elated.

But Arvella wasn't. We had no medical insurance, and now—no savings for the birth of our baby.

"Don't worry, dear," I assured her. "The church board meets this week. They'll all love it. They'll reimburse me and pick up the payments!" She was not at all convinced.

The board's negative reaction shocked me. "Yes, it's very nice, Reverend Schuller. But you bought it without our consultation or approval. There are more important things we need and can't afford. Send it back, unless you can pay for it yourself." The decision was firm—and final.

I had made the decision. Now I would somehow, someway have to raise the money. The sculpture belonged at the church. It turned the garden with its green lawn and cool waters into an open air "chapel." Couples would be married there. Memorial services and small funerals would be held there too.

I prayed, "God, didn't you lead me into this? Remember how I prayed, 'What are You up to today? I want to be a part of it'? Now, Lord, please help me!"

Within the next thirty days I received unexpected money from a lecture. Another offer of money came from a publisher—they wanted me to write a book for them. So the money for the baby's delivery was replaced.

People flocked to see the sculpture and stopped to pray. And they knew it wasn't paid for, so some made unsolicited gifts. In twenty-four months the sculpture was paid for. It stands at the Crystal Cathedral today, over a quarter of a century later.

Hundreds of weddings and funerals have been held in that place of still waters and green grass under the California sun. Bas-reliefs of the Good Shepherd appear on medals, stationery, and greeting cards. It is now world famous.

It was an answer to prayer and became part of a special place where thousands of prayers would be prayed. The garden became a place of meditation!

Careful what you pray for. You may get it!

*Good morning, Lord!*
*What are You up to today?*
*Can I be a part of it?*
*Thank You. Amen.*

Yes, prayer is my soul's adventure with God.

Meditation is the level at which miracles begin to move mountains.

# ALLELUIA—
# ANYWAY!

*On your feet! It's time to stand up in prayers
of praise and thanksgiving!*

"GIVING THANKS ALWAYS FOR ALL THINGS TO GOD THE FATHER
IN THE NAME OF OUR LORD JESUS CHRIST."
— EPHESIANS 5:20 —

# Chapter 11

# From Pain to Praise

You're ready now to step up to the level of prayer that I call "second to the highest step"—"Alleluia!" prayer.

Call it Praise.

Call it Thanksgiving.

This is prayer where the whole self becomes open and ebullient. "Oh, magnify the LORD with me, / And let us exalt His name together" (Ps. 34:3). That's it! Our effervescent and charismatic friends have captured the Psalmist's enthusiasm on this level of prayer.

I usually stand when I pray on this happy or hope-filling level. In petition or intercession I may be on my knees. I may be seated or lying down in the "couch" position for meditation or two-way prayer.

But in praise? It's nearly impossible to stay sitting down!

On your feet! It's time to catch the fervor of the big score. The ball through the hoop! Touchdown! Across the finish line! The crowd is on its feet! The envelope is opened. The announcer reads, "And the winner is . . ." Prayers are answered! Arms are raised! People who have been touched are rejoicing! Pentecostals, here we come!

I didn't grow up in this "praise-full" tradition of the Christian faith and life. I was never exposed to Pentecostal or charismatic ministers in childhood, college, or seminary. That is not a part of the Dutch Reformed tradition or culture.

But when your soul is on an adventure with God, you have to

be humble enough to confess, "I don't know it all." Through several experiences—some of them when life was coming apart—with charismatic men and women, I learned what it really means to pray on the praise level.

# Free to Explore!

My openness to the "new Pentecostalism" was certainly aided by the California culture. Here the mental climate was open, free. Boundaries would and could be challenged. Creativity was applauded. This explained why cults, far-out New Age philosophies of religion, and nontraditional expressions and interpretations were not frowned upon. Quite different from New York, Holland and Grand Rapids, Michigan, or northwest Iowa.

This environment was dynamic, which is why I dared to start in a drive-in theater and why I dared to be sincerely ecumenical. I felt at home in the California culture, which encouraged me to experiment and be liberated within the responsible guidelines of my denomination. We were a creedal group, a denomination with church law. I would always respect that, for it allowed me great freedom to grow, to be innovative, to explore. Adventure was acceptable within sensible boundaries.

All I truly believed was that there is more to my faith than I had been exposed to in my tradition. I really respected tradition. For any practice and truth to survive from one generation to the next must mean there is something there that is true and works. I never did find myself to be a negative reactionary by battling tradition. But I early and always felt that there is *something more than our tradition*. And I felt free to explore as long as it did not rudely and arrogantly challenge the heart of the faith.

# Something More Than My Tradition

A Pentecostal preacher came to Orange County a few years after I started the church in Garden Grove. His name was Ralph Wilkerson. Clergy of many denominations were invited to his church to receive the "gift of tongues."

I attended, cautiously. But nothing happened to me. Not that I could tell. And that was okay. I was "saved." I was a Christian. I didn't sense a need for "tongues." I knew that Jesus Christ was my Savior. That was, I felt, good enough.

Then I read some interesting stories. An Episcopalian priest was in the charismatic movement. Then a Lutheran. Then a Dutch Reformed minister, Harold Bredesen.

The mainline Protestant theologians and ecclesiastical hierarchy were almost overwhelmingly negative toward the new Pentecostalism. They offered discreet warnings. "Be careful. If you get a reputation for *that*—'tongue speaking' or 'glossolalia'—you'll be labeled and be out of consideration for many, if not all, of the prestigious and large churches."

Well, that fear didn't bother me. I was committed to this little church I had started in a drive-in theater. I was here for life. I was a "lifer."

## An Exciting New Spiritual Reality!

Since Dr. Harold Bredesen was in the newly emerging "Pentecostalism" within my denomination, I arranged an appointment with him, alone, in my private office.

Before he stepped in, I prayed, all alone in the "Let's Connect!" two-way prayer mode:

| | |
|---|---|
| **Question:** | **"God, is there more to the Christian life than I have experienced or known?"** |
| **Answer:** | *Yes.* |
| **Question:** | **"Do you want me to be open in mind and heart to what Bredesen may say to me?"** |
| **Answer:** | *Yes. I have a deeper spiritual life for you. And you must be sincerely honest and open, allowing Me to do with you what I want so that you might become the minister I want you to be. Let him come in. I will be with the two of you. I will have control. Just relax and respond to My leading.* |

Dr. Bredesen came in. I sat in my office chair. He sat only a few feet away on the sofa to my right, with no desk or credenza between us. (I never wanted to look across my desk when I talked with someone. Just like I did not want a pulpit between me and my congregation. No furniture that becomes what is called in psychology a "distancing device." No one-upmanship here, please!)

Bredesen was impressive. Intelligent. Doctrinally solid. Ecclesiastically "upper crust" with his black suit, clergy vest, and white turn-around collar. Meeting him was like looking at a Roman Catholic priest, or an Episcopalian or Lutheran clergyman. It made an academic statement. You didn't wear that garb as a clergyman unless you were college-educated, seminary-trained, and licensed by the denomination.

These were the same reasons I chose to wear the collegiate gown with academic stole. I wanted to let the people know I had taken no shortcuts to the ministry. I had, however, chosen not to wear the clergy collar. I sensed that many people I wanted to reach had strong prejudices against Roman Catholicism. They also prejudged the authenticity of the Bible as a "Holy Book." But they were impressed with a secular university degree. Robes were worn at university graduations and also worn by judges in court. So the robe, without the collar, and without a Bible in my hand, was the strategic choice I made and still do.

Harold was so respectable. We discussed the "glossolalia," speaking in tongues, deeply, thoroughly. He was persuasive without trying to sell or convert me. I sat and asked questions. And I listened, all the while prayerfully asking God to control my reactions and my responses.

Suddenly, sharply, clearly I found myself at the edge of a mental state called "deep relaxation." I was being mesmerized by the white collar.

"Harold," I said, waking myself up a bit, "I'm not going to ask for the gift of tongues while you sit here with me. If I do get the gift, I want to believe in it honestly. Permanently. I must never be tempted to discredit it as human manipulation. When you leave, I'll pray alone. God can give the gift to me if He wants to. I'm totally open to His

Holy Spirit. God has promised to take control of my soul. I want that."

Harold left. I was alone with God. I prayed, "Do you want me to speak in tongues? If so, here are my lips. Here is my tongue. Lord, I really feel the reality of a transcendent power and presence in this room and in my life that I now truly believe is the Holy Spirit. I'm yours, Holy Spirit. Do what You will with me."

I waited. And waited. I tried to articulate sounds that could have been "speaking in tongues." What happened I shall record as honestly as I can.

I was mentally consumed by, what to me, was a clear message from God: *I do not need to have you speak in an unknown tongue. I could do this for you. But I want to give you a gift of tongues in a language that can be understood by the people who are not believers. You are being given and you are receiving a gift that will never leave you. I am your Holy Spirit, and I will tumble out words that will impress the unbelievers. I know your audience better than you do. You will be intuitively, instinctively, impulsively articulate. You will, yourself, be shocked at sentences that will never enter your mind until your ears hear them coming out of your mouth.*

I was overwhelmed by the God-presence I felt. I trusted that message. God alone was in control of my moment, my mind, my heart, and my tongue!

My soul's adventure with God had brought me to an exciting new world of spiritual reality to which I had never been connected before.

❧

Thirty years later I testify that I have often heard unplanned, unexpected words coming from my mouth. I know it when I hear it. It is the Holy Spirit. I have absolutely no basis to doubt it. And when the words come, I hear them with surprise—and with respect for the Lord who has never stopped giving me this gift.

Some might call this gift a type of intuition. I know better!

I would challenge, in my life, the world's leading psychiatrists, Dr. Karl Mennenger and Dr. Viktor Frankl: "What's intuition?" They both would answer, "We really don't know what it is. But you, Dr. Schuller, are a most intuitive person."

So I tend to trust my intuitive feelings and to never, ever react to these positive impulses from the Holy Spirit in a cavalier manner.

## The Gift of Words

Another personal miracle with my "gift of tongues."

I was invited to speak to three thousand business people at a Hilton hotel in Chicago. It was a commercial lecture, for which I charge a high fee. This fee and all of my other speaking fees, amounting to nearly a quarter of a million dollars a year, go to my nonprofit ministry to ministers, which for more than twenty-five years has sustained my efforts to inspire, affirm, and encourage ministers to build healthy, growing churches worldwide.

"Thanks for coming, Dr. Schuller," the president of the Chicago convention said as he met me backstage. "But don't go up there and tell jokes, and don't smile like you do on television. Half the people in this audience are going into bankruptcy this year. They're going through tough times. You wouldn't tell jokes or laugh when you go to a funeral, would you?"

He didn't know it, but he had just blown my act. Then through the curtains I heard the master of ceremonies introduce me, ending with "and now let's welcome Dr. Schuller."

I had no idea what I would say as I mounted the steps. I prayed, and I suddenly remembered what I'd been taught by the Hope College Speech Department more than thirty years ago! This memory came "out of the blue," a fantastic, instant, creative answer to prayer: "If you ever get caught onstage and don't know what to say, play the dramatic pause for all it's worth."

I paced the stage silently, like a prowling tiger. I stared at the audience, walking slowly from one end to the other. The crowd became so quiet you could hear a pin drop.

"I hear you're in trouble," I heard myself say. Then I remembered further advice the speech professor gave us: "If, in your dramatic pause, you can't think of anything to say, just tell them your story." (Thank you for these reminders, Holy Spirit.)

"Let me tell you my story," I said. For the first thirty minutes of that forty-five-minute speaking engagement I shared my story of troubled times. The Depression and childhood poverty on the farm. The tornado. The fire. My daughter's accident on the motorcycle and my wife's cancer.

And then I heard myself say, "Now let me tell you what I've learned from my tough times!" I paused. I paced. I stared them in the eye. I was trapped. I had painted myself into a corner onstage. I had no idea what I'd learned from these "tough times." I had to deliver. *But I was not alone.* God was with me. He had given me the "gift of tongues"! I heard myself bellow out the sentence:

**"Tough times never last, but tough people do!"**

The audience leaped to their feet. They were blown away! So was I! I had never heard that line before anywhere!

"That's a powerful line," I said.

"I don't want to forget it. I've got to write it down." And quickly I almost ran to the podium and wrote it down. The audience laughed and applauded.

That sentence became a book, my first book to make the bestseller list of the *New York Times*! More than a million copies would be sold. And countless more in many foreign languages. It was a gift from God, through me, to more people than I'll ever know. Again and again and again and again, I have experienced what I truly believe is this unique gift of the Holy Spirit.

Thank you, Harold Bredesen. And thank You, Lord.

# The "Alleluia" Room

My "gift of the Holy Spirit" would also prepare me to meet some great new friends in Christian ministry half a world away.

I was a guest speaker at the largest Presbyterian church in Korea, where ministers had gathered in a private room to greet me.

There was only one woman present. In Korean culture, women were not invited. But she had read my books, prayerfully decided to practice Possibility Thinking, and boldly entered the room uninvited! She got to the front of the line and spoke to me. I was impressed with her courage, her sincerity, her intelligence.

"My name is Mrs. Cho," she said. "My husband, David, is pastor of the Full Gospel Church in Seoul. You must come and preach there the next time you come to Korea. The Lord sent me, a Pentecostal, here today to hear you and to tell you that He wants you to speak in my husband's church the next time you're in this country."

She had no idea how prophetic she was. Neither did I! I would later speak at that church and then endure one of the most heart-rending, horrific tragedies I would ever experience. God knew how I would need the ministry of that church desperately, urgently, in a sorrow-filled day to come.

I told Mrs. Cho I would come and speak.

"Thank you, Dr. Schuller. You'll never know how helpful you were to my husband."

A copy of my book, *Move Ahead with Possibility Thinking,* had found its way to Korea and into the hands of Cho, who at this time was following God's guidance to build a great church. Tough times hit him. Discouragement plagued him.

Later he would tell me, "That book, Dr. Schuller, renewed my faith and made me a Possibility Thinker. And that saved my ministry and my church in hard times."

On my next trip to Korea, I met Dr. David Yonggi Cho and sat beside him on the platform of what was already the largest church in the world. I had never before been invited by a Pentecostal to preach a sermon in a Pentecostal church. What courage he had to invite me, and what courage I had to accept! God was in charge of both of our lives and ministries.

Never before had I been in a "praise-filled" service. "Alleluia," the people sang. "Alleluia," the people chanted in liberated joy. It was a life-changing experience for me. The Holy Spirit's presence, peace, power, and pleasure were there. "Alleluia."

I returned to my hotel room. The telephone rang. It was the most painful call I would ever get.

"Bob," it was my chief aide, Michael Nason, calling. "Your daughter Carol has been in a terrible accident. She's in the emergency room at St. Joseph Hospital in Sioux City, Iowa. The doctor wants to talk to you. Here's the number."

I wrote it down.

Mike explained how Carol had been on the back of her cousin's motorcycle when they had collided at high speed with an oncoming car. The helmet she was wearing probably saved her life. But they were going to amputate her left leg. I almost fainted.

I called the doctor. "First the good news, Dr. Schuller. We have saved her life. She took seventeen units of blood. But we have to amputate the leg."

Stunned, I replied, "We'll catch the first flight home."

I called Dr. Cho. He said he'd find seats on the next plane back to America. "Pack," he said. "We'll pray."

Three hours later, Pastor Cho with his precious wife, Grace, along with Pastor Cho's chief aide and his wife, Mr. and Mrs. Cha, sat with Arvella and me in a private waiting room at Seoul International Airport.

We all held hands. "All things work together for good to those who love God and keep His commandments," I heard Pastor Cho say. I had preached that so often and had always believed it so sincerely. Now for the first time I wondered, *Is it really true?* But I said nothing.

"Let's pray," Cho said. Our wet eyes closed. And I heard these godly, positive Pentecostals murmuring over and over, "Alleluia." "Alleluia." "Thank you, Lord, for being with us in this terrible time." "Thank you, Lord!" "Alleluia." "For getting seats on this plane. Alleluia." "Thank you, Lord, that Carol's life has been saved."

I had entered another room in the mansion of prayer in which my soul had never been before in its adventure with God! Call the room "Prayers of Praise and Thanksgiving." Call it the "Alleluia" room.

The airport executive came and ushered us on the plane. We said our good-byes.

We sat together, Arvella and I, holding hands. She stared wet-eyed through the window as the plane waited to take off. The stewardess sat seat-belted right in front of me, her legs crossed. Two legs. Two feet. *Carol has only one foot now,* I thought. *Two ankles. One of Carol's is gone. Two legs. Carol has only one leg left.*

The plane took off—strong, loud, fast. The seat belt sign went off. The stewardess stood up—and walked. *Carol will never again be able to do that.* The thought—horrific—consumed me. I could not hold it back. I wanted to bawl out loud. I had to get to the bathroom.

I unbuckled my belt, went to the toilet, locked the door, and lost it! Crying is simple, silent weeping. Bawling is uncontrollable wailing and moaning. I bawled.

In the midst of my anguish I heard once again the Korean Christians singing and chanting, "Alleluia." And sweetly, strangely, I fashioned my lips to shape the wailing sounds into the words, "Alleluia." "Alleluia." Again and again. First, loudly. Then, softer. Last, only in sacred, serene whispers: "Alleluia."

I was high on the steps in the throne room of prayer. I don't know how long it lasted. I only remember I praised God.

Then and there my soul was lifted. For the first time in my life I discovered the peace and the power in praise.

*Flashback:* Mrs. Cho is meeting me long ago in the Presbyterian church and saying, "Dr. Schuller, the Lord has sent me here to tell you that the next time you come to Korea you must come and preach in our church!"

Yes, I did go there to preach. But, more important, I went there to learn that when life starts to come apart, you need to rush to a special level of prayer. There's a word on the door of that private holy place: *Alleluia!*

# Chapter 12

# From Gratitude
# to Generosity

Through our Possibility Thinking in our time of pain, we will climb to the "Alleluia!" level of praise-packed prayer.

But there is a painless path to this lofty level. It's the habit of praying daily, "Thank You, Lord."

Thanksgiving! Our thoughts and actions of sincere gratitude delight the heart of our glorious, giving God.

I am a man who in his sixth decade has much to be thankful for. Here are some milestones:

The publication of this, my thirtieth book, in the year 1995.

The fortieth anniversary of the church—1955–1995.

The twenty-fifth anniversary of the Robert Schuller Institute for Successful Preaching—1970–1995.

The twenty-fifth anniversary of *The Hour of Power*—1970–1995.

The fifteenth anniversary of the opening of the Crystal Cathedral—1980–1995.

The fifth anniversary of my first sermon preached in the Soviet Union—1989–1994.

And *most important:*

The forty-fifth anniversary of the wedding of Robert Harold Schuller to Arvella DeHaan—1950–1995.

That's the important anniversary. None of the others would have been possible if she had not been at my side. She is my encourager, constructive critic, coach, and manager.

"He who finds a wife finds a good thing" (Prov. 18:22). I did. Thank You, Lord!

## They Know the Real Me

"What's the real Robert Schuller like?" I've been asked since I lost my privacy and became a public personage. "We know your image, but what is the real *you?*"

"You're asking the right question," I always answer. "I'll answer as honestly as I can. But if you want to know the real me, ask those who have known me the longest and seen me at my worst. They are my family, my wife and our five children."

They've seen me at my best and my worst.

In family prayers, where we've always held hands and prayed as a family around the table—at morning breakfast and evening dinner.

I was so honored when our firstborn child, Sheila, wrote a biography of me and chose the title *My Father—My Friend.* We are all the best of friends.

All five children are beautiful Christians. I know I could not have been such a successful father without my wife, Arvella.

Every night of my early years, I prayed, "Make me a preacher."

And then every night my wife and I prayed earnestly on Level Three: "Please bless our children with the happy faith we enjoy." All five children today love Jesus Christ. They live blessed lives in nice houses, with wonderful spouses and adorable children.

As I publish this book, I submit for the record that prayer—faithful, positive, daily prayer—for each and all of our children is a matter of indisputable record.

My marriage and family have been so blessed that I cannot, will not, must not fail to say that I am certain they reflect the truth that *real prayer really works.*

Yes, all five children faced their own unique problems and troubles. All five had to—and did—make personal decisions about God, Jesus Christ, the family, marriage, and morality. They're all persons—not puppets.

# Financially Blessed

Arvella and I insisted firmly that each child would have to leave home upon graduation from high school to attend a Christian college. My income from book royalties made it possible to offer a college education to each of them.

Only Carol did not attend a Christian college. She went instead to a handicapped ski village in Colorado, where she learned to be an independent adult, not depending on her family to do things for her. What an education she had! Her years in Colorado equipped her with an "I can do" attitude she would need for the rest of her life.

I am so thankful that through the expensive years of educating our five children these royalties have sustained us.

ॐ

I am also so thankful to my denomination, which set minimum salaries in small churches that would still be enough to comfortably provide for the pastor and family. If the income from a small church wouldn't meet this minimum requirement, then the denomination was, by church law, obligated to supplement the pastor's income to meet this minimum. Always they have cared for their pastors.

I started in the ministry at the minimum salary and stayed there for years and years. After thirty-five years, when our church became the largest church in the denomination, my salary equaled, but would never surpass, the salary of Norman Vincent Peale in our oldest and second-largest church, The Marble Collegiate Church of the Reformed Church in America, in New York City.

In contrast to this were Jim and Tammy Bakker, who came up through a denomination that permitted churches to pay their ministers a tithe of the church's income. For many, this was woefully inadequate. If the church had, in the 1980s for instance, an income of one hundred thousand dollars, their full-time pastor's income was only ten thousand dollars.

Enter Jim Bakker. If the income of the church grew to one million dollars, a year's salary could be one hundred thousand dollars. No one thought to put a ceiling on the system. At its peak, Bakker's ministry had an income reported at well over one hundred million dollars a year! He could have claimed the right to accept a tithe—or ten million dollars. He never did, of course, but his personal returns were large enough to create a scandal.

When the Bakker scandals emerged, I was put under the cloud simply because I was a pastor on television. Investigative reporters never stopped to analyze the different structures of different denominations.

But investigative reporters were never educated in denominational law and order to know these things. Nor, in their paranoid suspicions, did they ever cease to suspect that I was inappropriately salaried.

"So live that when you die you'll have proven your critics to have been liars," someone said.

Prayers of thanksgiving generate gratitude. Alleluia.

# An "Alleluia" Prayer of Thanksgiving

Arvella. Many times she found lumps in her breast. Always they were benign. So, the last time, neither she nor I was concerned. She went alone to the doctor, a dear family friend, and had the lump removed. It was instantly checked.

"Benign again, Arvella," he said.

Two days later the phone rang.

"Arvella, can I talk to Bob?" It was our friend, the doctor.

"Hi, Ralph! This is Bob."

"Bob, we sent the lump from Arvella's breast for further tests. I wanted to make sure that the section of lump that tested benign would not mislead us. So I sent the entire lump to be checked out fully, and I just got a report back. They did find some malignant cells."

I was stunned. Silent.

"Now that I've told you, Bob, I'll talk to Arvella."

The best advice was followed. A mastectomy was scheduled and carried out.

Both of us prayed "Alleluia!" prayers filled with thanksgiving:

"Thank You, Lord, for the doctor who left nothing to early and incomplete tests."

"Thank You, Lord, that cancer was found early and that it will, we believe, be cured completely."

"Thank You, Lord, that Arvella can live without a breast. Thank You that there was no cancer found in her lymph nodes. That she is not losing a life-sustaining body organ such as her kidneys or liver."

"Thank You, Lord, that the scars can be corrected through reconstructive surgery and covered by her clothing."

"Thank You, Lord, for her faith! And her commitment and passion to serve in all the great, glorious, generous, gracious, and good works she'll do for Jesus Christ the rest of her life."

"Thank You, Lord, that the loss of a breast will not in any way restrain or restrict her compulsion and capability to be a fun-loving grandmother to all her grandchildren—those alive today and those still unborn."

"Thank You, Lord, that the loss of her breast will not make any difference to the beautiful, fulfilling, satisfying, intimate, and mutually encouraging relationship we have as husband and wife."

That was fifteen years ago. Did these prayers of thanksgiving release endorphins to contribute to what has been a blessed cure?

Special blessings come to the positive-praying, positive-living, and positive-expecting believer. And that's an indisputable, scientific, proven fact!

Thank You, Lord!

## Caught Smuggling Bibles!

The Soviet Union—1968.

It was no secret that for years in the U.S.S.R., religion was considered an enemy of the state. It was against the law to read the Bible in your home. Believers were persecuted mercilessly. In fact, I came face-to-face with the opposition to faith when I agreed to smuggle Bibles into Russia.

I had agreed to undertake this covert mission because I believed that God's Word was direly needed by the people of the Soviet Union. I believed that it was worth risking my safety to deliver God's Word to these persecuted believers.

I am not by nature a heroic man. Consequently, I was extremely nervous going through customs.

I had packed the Bibles as instructed. My traveling companion, Ike Eichenberger, was also carrying concealed Bibles. He was ahead of me in the customs line. The border guard carefully searched his suitcase. I dared not look at Ike, suspecting that the guards would sense my fear. They found nothing.

Inwardly, I sighed. They hadn't found Ike's Bibles; they probably wouldn't find mine.

Nevertheless, it was with sweaty palms that I handed the official my passport. He looked at my passport a long time. He read my name and studied my face.

Then he opened my suitcase and lifted the carefully folded piles of clothing. Suddenly, his hand stopped. He pried. He prodded. He discovered my carefully hidden treasure. I had been caught! What would he do to me?

He held up a handful of Bibles and called excitedly to his colleagues. They conversed furtively in Russian. Every now and then they would look in my direction. One of them said in broken English, "You must wait."

After finding my Bibles, they were suspicious of Ike too. They recalled his suitcase, and a more careful search uncovered his stash as well.

I was not naïve. I knew that this would not be tolerated. The Bibles were confiscated. We were given a stern warning and then, miracle of miracles, we were allowed to enter the country anyway!

I was overwhelmed by the beauty of the Soviet Union. I visited every museum I could find.

In my search to see and learn as much as I could about the Soviet Union, I heard about the Museum of Atheism. I was shocked but intrigued. I felt that I had to see the museum in order to understand the State's fear of a belief system.

I called our guide. "Have you heard of the Museum of Atheism?"

"Yes, of course!"

"Would you take us to see it?"

"It would be my pleasure."

I had no idea what to expect. I was surprised and saddened to see that the Museum of Atheism was housed in an abandoned church. This temple of God had been transformed into a house of unbelief. The museum hailed proponents of Communism and atheists in displays entitled "Heroes of the State." Heroes included such people as Lenin, Castro, and Marx. Our guide enthusiastically told us about each of these men and detailed how they had helped liberate people from "the opiate of religion."

Then she took us into another room. On the wall were similar profiles, pictures, newspaper clippings, etc. These displays detailed the lives of men and women under the heading "Enemies of the State." There were pictures of men I knew, like Billy Graham, Martin Luther King, the Pope, and *Robert Schuller.*

Robert Schuller! I looked again. Sure enough, there was a picture and a magazine article that told about our ministry and the unique church I had founded, a walk-in, drive-in church. I blanched. I felt that same fear I had felt when the border guards discovered the Bibles.

Our guide looked at my picture, then she looked at me. Then she looked at the heading "Enemies of the State."

Without a word, she led us back to our hotel and left us in the lobby.

I was worried. I was in a hostile country where I had already been caught breaking the law. Now I was identified in a prominent museum as an Enemy of the State.

Ike and I retreated to our room. It felt like the safest thing to do.

The next day we flew from Leningrad to Luvov. When we stepped off the plane, a man approached us and said, "Follow me. Don't ask any questions."

Fear was in Ike's eyes as well as mine as we followed this mystery man. He put us in the back seat of a car and drove us through the sleeping city. We had no idea where he was taking us.

Were we his captives?

Were we being taken to a prison?

Would my wife ever know what had happened to me?

We drove silently out of the city and through the countryside. The trees loomed dark and ominous along the country roads. The farther we got from civilization, the more concerned I became. Needless to say, I prayed that God would spare my friend and me.

After an hour's drive through the Russian woods, we turned onto a side road. Lights shone through the trees. As we got closer, it became clear that the lights outlined a runway. A plane stood poised, ready for takeoff. The driver pulled up close to the gangway and said gruffly, "Get out!"

Another mystery man opened the car door for us, pointed up the gangway to the open door of the plane, and said, "Get on!"

We didn't feel that we were in a position to argue, so we did as we were told.

Where was this plane headed?

What was our destination? Siberia?

The engine of the plane began to roar. The body of the plane began to rumble. Soon the thrust forced us back into the seat, and we soared into the black sky.

Without the sun to guide us, it was impossible to know what direction we were headed. We could have been going south, toward Egypt, or north, toward Siberia, or west. Could we be going west? Could this plane be taking us out of the Soviet Union? It seemed like a slim hope, but that one hopeful thought led to another.

Of course, they wouldn't risk kidnapping us, holding us here against our will, would they? After all, we were citizens of the United States. We had rights. Didn't we?

We flew for hours. Suddenly the plane began to rumble. I had flown enough to recognize the sound of landing gear being lowered into position. We were going to land. But where?

Sure enough, the engine shifted gears, the plane tilted downward, and tips of trees became visible. Lights, like those of a village, shone in the distance. Wherever we were, we were near some semblance of civilization. It was the village of Kiev. We were driven to a railroad station and put onboard a train, which would take us out of the Soviet Union—to the free West—Vienna.

Thank You, Lord. Alleluia—after all!

## "Am I Asking Too Much, Dad?"

My oldest daughter, Sheila, sat at the corner table in our kitchen with me. She was heartbroken. She had just been jilted by a man she trusted and had hoped might become her husband. His treatment was rude, crude, and very hurtful.

She cried.

So did I.

"Dad, all I want is a man who will treat me like a *precious gem*. Like you treat Mom." Her shoulders dropped. Tears rolled out, and anger changed her face from sweet attractiveness into the tragic look of undeserved sadness, grief, hurt, disappointment, and pessimism. "Is that really asking too much, Dad?"

I broke down. Then I jumped up to hug her. Holding her tightly, I said, "No, Sheila, that's not too much to ask."

I don't recall all of our words, but we prayed on the "alleluia!" level. I was so thankful that she knew God's love for her and she was surrounded by the love of her family. She was true to her commitment to Jesus Christ and the Ten Commandments.

I thanked God that she was a serious, sensible student. She would proudly receive her bachelor's degree and go on to find great fulfillment in her ministry as a public school teacher.

I thanked God that He was here, hearing our prayer and planning a beautiful future for her. I could hear Him saying to her, "For I know the plans I have for you, says the Lord. They are plans for good and not for evil, to give you a future and a hope" (Jer. 29:11, TLB).

Two years later, Arvella and I were in Hong Kong. The telephone rang. It was Sheila, in America.

"Dad, how does February sound for a wedding?"

"Oh, God, thank You! Really, Sheila? Jim asked you to become his *wife!*" I could sense her joy all the way across the Pacific.

"Yes, Dad, and I know Jim will always treat me like a precious gem."

## "Bob, You'll Have to Pay the Bill."

The day before Sheila's wedding, I told one of the church's elders, who was a medical doctor: "I'm afraid I'll lose it and cry when I start to walk her down the aisle."

"No problem, Bob. I'll give you a medication that will prevent that."

"But then I won't really feel the joy," I objected. "I'll pray instead," I answered. "And trust the Lord."

Sheila was gorgeous in her white gown. She was radiant with joy. We waited at the back and watched her sisters walk in to take their place as bridesmaids.

Just then the wedding march broke out, and I felt the tears welling up, but God was answering my prayer. Into my mind came an idea, a thought that would keep me from crying and still allow me to freely feel the grand emotions of the day. The thought?

*Just remember, Bob. You'll have to pay the bill.*

I laughed.

Lord, what a healing, helpful sense of humor you have!

## Paying the Bill the Second Time!

Later I had the same joy when Jeanne married.

Jeanne, our third child, was seven years old when a new baby sister was born into our family, followed by still another baby sister two years later. Where for seven years she had been the "baby darling," now Jeanne was sandwiched in between.

Jeanne grew up with a very independent personality, excelling in academics. So when it was time for her to graduate and select her college, I was disappointed that she did not choose my alma mater like her older brother and sister had done, but she instead applied and was accepted to Wheaton College in Illinois.

Jeanne had a tough time there, not academically but with the constant criticism about her dad building the Crystal Cathedral and spending so much money that "should be used for missions." This was hard for her to take, but she persevered—through faith and the positive-thinking attitude that she had learned so well at home. She also chose to volunteer for her friend, Bill Hybels, who, with his wife, was starting a new church in a theater, much like her dad had done.

Then one summer she signed up for the Wheaton College Summer Holy Land Study Program. And there, on the hot and dusty road to Jericho, she met Paul.

Three years after her graduation, I walked her, as a beautiful bride, down the aisle of the Crystal Cathedral to her handsome groom, Paul.

## "Here Comes the Bride"—the Third Bill!

The whole church had prayed that Carol would be able to attend her sister Sheila's wedding, but signs indicated she wouldn't make it. A horrible infection was threatening further amputation, perhaps even the whole thigh, which had been broken so badly. Now, suddenly, a new drug was available! The doctors would try it. It worked wonders! Overnight! She was finally cured! She could go home and attend the wedding.

Now she was at Sheila's wedding. Her long blonde hair and her floor-length gown made her a stunning bridesmaid with her sisters Jeanne Anne and Gretchen Joy.

"There is no way you can wear a prosthesis yet," the doctor had told her. "If you want to walk down that aisle at your sister's wedding, it will have to be on crutches."

"Someday, Dad, I'll walk that aisle in a bride's dress—without crutches and without a limp."

I gulped. I remembered the hurtful, hope-threatening question I had asked myself just seven months ago on that long, agonizing flight home from South Korea. The thought had cut through my mind like a sharp knife. *Will Carol ever find a husband? Would a man fall in love with and marry her even though she has only one leg?* I worried. I prayed.

God heard.

It happened.

One of the best, most handsome men God ever made would meet Carol, pray and praise God with her, and fall in love with her.

The day came when Carol walked down the aisle on her special day.

"Here comes the bride." The organ music filled the cathedral, and Carol walked in without crutches and almost without a limp.

And I didn't cry this time either!

## Bride Number Four—the Last Bill!

Gretchen, our last child, had numerous boyfriends, but none measured up to her standards. All of us agreed.

One night, after returning from a date, she announced in frustration, "That's it; I'm not dating any guy until my next birthday," which was nearly a year away. Gretchen asked us to pray that she would know the one God had chosen for her.

We watched and prayed as she turned down some nice young men. There was one particularly nice guy named Jim whom all of us liked, but Gretchen refused to date him.

Jim, however, was persistent. He would not take a no from Gretchen. He kept sending her flowers and encouraging her in her schoolwork.

When Gretchen's birthday happened almost a year later, so did love! Gretchen said, "Dad, I'm in love. You better start saving some extra money, because you'll have to pay for another wedding this October."

Alleluia! Thank You, God!

And no tears!

# Learning Together, Praying Together

1995. My wife and I, both healthy and happy, are looking forward to celebrating our forty-fifth wedding anniversary. It will be a crowded party!

All of our five, happily married children, each with their wonderful Christian spouses, and all of the seventeen grandchildren will be together.

Don't ever try to tell me that the true story of my soul's adventure with God would have unfolded so gloriously if we hadn't *all* been adventuring together with God in prayer—every day, every step of the way.

Of course, we have had our share of disagreements and arguments. That's natural in a growing family. A family is not a watch in which all the parts of the mechanism run smoothly day after day. Can you imagine if all the parts of the watch were growing?

That's a family! One day everything runs smoothly; the next day we are at odds with each other. Why? Because we are growing! Seven people, in our home, all programmed to be Possibility Thinkers, learning together, working together, and growing together. We *had* to pray together in order to live together.

A Christmas gift from Gretchen (now twenty-eight) last year was a collage of photos of her and me together. On the back of the picture frame, Gretchen had taped a note she had written to me when she was a teenager. This keepsake is a tribute to my soul's adventure with God.

**Dad, I'm so sorry for arguing with you last night. I felt terrible about it, and I wanted to apologize before I went to bed. "Don't let the sun go down on our anger."**

No, I'm not angry, although I was. But I still feel that I want to say I'm sorry. I *love you* very much. I just want you to know that.

Last night at youth group we had to say who we would like to be if we could be somebody else. My response was, next to Jesus, I would want to be *my dad,* because he is a positive thinker for the Lord. He has done many good things for many good people, especially *me!* Thanks, Dad, for being who you are and making *me—me!*

Love, Gretchen

Thank You, Lord.
Alleluia!

# MAKE ME A BLESSING!

*"God loves you and so do I."*
*I am blessed—to be a blessing.*

"AND YOU SHALL BE CALLED THE REPAIRER OF THE BREACH,
THE RESTORER OF STREETS TO DWELL IN."
— ISAIAH 58:12 —

# Chapter 13

# The Greatest Prayer

Praise while in pain. Thanksgiving in the wake of hurt. Could any level of prayer be nobler, higher, holier than Alleluia? Yes!

You have reached the last step, the highest, holiest level of prayer.

At every point on your soul's adventure God has listened to you.

Level One: When you dreamed the dream and prayed positively, He heard your heart.

Level Two: When you took the next step and called out for "Help!" God answered you and started to turn you into the person He wanted you to be. He *saved* you.

Level Three: When you pleaded on your knees for His grace and blessing on a friend, on a dear relative—even on an enemy. God listened to you.

Level Four: When you only asked Him questions. Then waited humbly, listening for an answer. "I'm open!" you said. He spoke softly to your soul, and you knew it was your God!

Level Five: When you were alone, in meditation, and surrendered your soul to His Spirit's power, control, and peace. He connected. He touched you.

Level Six: When you cried in a crisis, and the loss was more than anything you had ever known. You simply gave praise and thanksgiving and cried, "Alleluia, anyway!" And He blessed you beyond all human expectations.

Now, you're at the top—prayer at Level Seven, *Blessing*! This is a prayer in which you will be able to share your achievements. Now you will move from success to significance.

This is the greatest prayer—that you'll be an *answer* to prayer!

When I "discovered" this level, I was past my sixtieth year. For more than a half century God had been at work answering my first prayer. But He wasn't finished with me yet. He had to teach me that there was a higher, holier, more honorable level of prayer than I had ever really known! The Prayer of Blessing.

It happened at an autograph party only a few years ago. But before I tell that story, I need to show how God was shaping my understanding of His gospel. He knew I needed a fresh experience with Jesus Christ.

## Prepared to Be a Blessing

Arvella and I were given tickets to see the musical *Man of La Mancha.* The man of La Mancha sings "To Dream the Impossible Dream." He meets Aldonza, the prostitute, and calls her, "My lady! And I give you a new name—Dulcinea." I suddenly see a new, fresh paradigm of the gospel.

The knight? A representation of Christ.

The prostitute? The knight sees her not as she is, but as she can be! Not as a whore—but as a lady!

It was like Dr. Peale had preached in the drive-in years before, "If Jesus were here, would He tell you what lost sinners you all are? No! He'd tell you 'Follow me. Here's what you can become!'"

Sin? It's breaking God's rules.

Sin? We're conceived and born in it.

Sin? It's lack of faith in the positive possibilities that God wants us to experience.

Sin? It's rejecting instead of respecting and responding to the invitation to become a beautiful child of God.

Suddenly, in my seat, watching *Man of La Mancha,* the message I am to preach to the world becomes clear.

*The Madrid conference*—"Faith, Hope, Love."

*My childhood theology*—Children are born sinners. They may not be bad; they're just not believers.

*My Frankl exposure*—Take away dignity and you lose all meaning.

Watching *Man of La Mancha,* my mind spun from one question to another.

*How do we preach against sin in such a way that we bless the sinner to become a saint, instead of cursing the sinner to despair in his reality? How should I preach to get people to believe that they are created with the potential and possibility of being born again as children of God?*

The play continues. The harlot enters an empty stage. She has been raped—the ultimate human insult and indignity. She's hysterical. The knight sees her and calls out, "My Lady! Dulcinea!"

She screams! She recoils, the same way unbelieving sinners reject and rebel against Christ's call to become saints. She screams, "Don't call me a lady. I was born in a ditch by a mother who left me there, naked and cold and too hungry to cry. I never blamed her. I'm sure she left hoping that I'd have the good sense to die. Look at me. I'm no lady. I'm only a kitchen slut, reeking with sweat. A strumpet men use and forget. Don't call me Dulcinea. I am only Aldonza and I am nothing at all!"

Filled with shame, poisoned by guilt, and hopeless without dignity, Aldonza runs off into the darkness.

"But you are my lady, Dulcinea," the knight calls out to the fleeing wretch.

I had a fresh vision of Christ calling to the lost soul. "But you are My child. You are a child of God. He loves you, even if you are a lost soul. Find and follow the faith God has for you. You'll be born again and turned into a beautiful, 'blessed to be a blessing' soul."

By now I'm weeping in my theater seat. I see Jesus Christ as the Knight, the beautiful Redeemer.

The curtain rises on the last act. The knight is dying—like Jesus—condemned as an outcast, a crazy person. The knight's heart is broken, like Christ's heart was broken on the Cross.

To the knight's dying bed comes a lady. Beautiful in mantilla and lace. A heavenly choir sings. She prays.

He opens his eyes. "Who are you?" he asks.

She rises, stands erect, and answers, "My name? My name is Dulcinea!"

Aldonza has been reborn. She has repented and has been born again and transformed! The unbeliever has become a believer. The sinner has become a saint.

The impossibility thinker has become a Possibility Thinker! What really changed her? The knight's belief in what she could and would become! "I am not what I think I am. I am not what you think I am. I am what I think you think I am."

God has made me a preacher. I am ready to preach good news, the gospel for the whole wide world! Now I know I can be a blessing.

❧

*Make me a blessing, Make me a blessing—*
*Out of my life may Jesus shine;*
*Make me a blessing, O Savior, I pray,*
*Make me a blessing to someone today.*
                              *(Ira B. Wilson)*

We sang that chorus in the college quartet.

I prayed that prayer for years.

God has now prepared me. The prayer is answered. His plan will unfold. I am made ready by His grace and Spirit to be a blessing.

## The Prayer of Blessing

The time had arrived. I was about to experience prayer on the seventh level.

"I'll never do that again," I said with deep emotional fatigue. "Last week was unbelievable." Arvella sipped the Monday morning cup of coffee and smiled. Only eight days before, she had kissed me good-bye on a Sunday afternoon and watched my bags being loaded in the car that came to take me to a private jet rented by my publisher.

"We're proud and excited to have this new book, Dr. Schuller. We have to maximize exposure so the people who can be helped will know it's out," I had been told.

The publisher had outlined an unprecedented campaign to promote my newest book on the beatitudes of Jesus Christ.

The title: *The Be-Happy Attitudes.*

The plan? Fifteen autograph parties in fifteen states in five days! I would have an hour and a half in each store.

It looked great on paper. They sold me on it. I agreed. I did it.

In every city there were people waiting for me to arrive. When I landed at the airport, a waiting car took me to the back door of a bookstore in a mall.

The plan worked beautifully. The book made the top-ten nonfiction best-seller list in the *New York Times.* It was a super-successful strategy. But it really wiped me out.

"Never again, Arvella," I repeated.

She smiled. She understood. She agreed.

## A Look, A Word, A Touch

A few years later came the infamous television scandals. The same week that the story broke on Jimmy Swaggart's relationship with a prostitute, another new book of mine came out: *Success Is Never Ending—Failure Is Never Final.*

Bookstores suddenly pulled my newest release from their front windows. All television ministers were peppered with the ashes that fell from the eruption of the volcanic story. Jimmy Swaggart added to the earlier scandal of Jim and Tammy Bakker. My new book was lost in the cloud. I was suddenly standing in the shadows of suspicion. I refused to go out and sign books. I retreated.

Months became a year—and another year. Another new book was finished.

"Dr. Schuller," the publisher said, "you've been cleared of all suspicion. You've got to go out and meet your readers, friends, and fans again. The book deserves it. Please let us put a week of autograph parties together."

In a weak moment, I broke my promise to my wife and said, "Okay!"

Now here I was with several hundred people standing in line before me at a Waldenbooks in a mall. They stared, they waved, they smiled. I returned the waves and smiles as I groaned inside and wondered, *Can I possibly sign books for all these people?* It would have to be rushed. I had to get out of there in ninety minutes.

"Here's how we'll do it," the bookstore manager told me. "You'll sit at the table. On your left will be a clerk, who will greet the next person in line, take the book or books [many came with shopping bags full of my older books and apologetically asked me to sign all of them], open the book, and place it before you. Don't stop and visit with them, Dr. Schuller. Just sign it and pass it to the other clerk on your right. He'll close it, and hand it to them. You'll sign the next book before you. We'll have an assembly line.

"Just don't look up. Avoid eye contact. The clerks will do that and thank them.

"If you don't get hung up talking to them, I think we'll give everyone what they want and get you out of here in time to make the plane to the next city where people are already arriving."

I listened. I obeyed.

Monday night. The first autograph parties were behind me. I checked into my hotel room. I dressed for bed, dropped my head to the pillow, and was suddenly overwhelmed by a wave of guilt and depression.

It was time for some Level Four two-way prayer. I had some questions. I needed guidance. The following conversation took place between God and me. My lips spoke. My soul's inner ear listened for His still, small voice.

RHS: "Oh Lord, today's autograph parties were terrible. I feel awful. Why did I agree to do this?"

God: *I wanted you to do this. I made this decision and motivated you to agree to it.*

RHS: "But why do I feel so bad about it?"

God: *You're doing it wrong. You're not giving them what they came for.*

RHS: "But, God, I gave every one of them my autograph!" (I was arguing with God!)

God: *But that's not what they really came for,* God whispered back to my soul's inner ear.

RHS: "But that's what they were promised! That's what the publisher promised them in the newspaper ads! I gave them what I promised! Didn't I?"

God: *Yes—you gave them what you promised. But that is not what they really came for! They see you as My ambassador. They wanted a blessing through you from their God!*

RHS: I was stunned. I knew that was impossible. "But I don't have the time, Lord! If I even *look* at them, I'll be drawn into their lives. They'll start talking to me. I can't be rude!" I foolishly tried to "inform" the Lord. "Five hundred people divided by ninety minutes—that's nearly six people every sixty seconds!"

God: *Try it! Don't worry about "finishing the line." Give every person a blessing. Give every person a look—lock eyes; a word—say something—let* Me *say something to them through your lips, eyes, and face. And give each person a touch—My touch!*

RHS: "Dear Lord, I'll try."

The prayer "conversation" had ended. I was silenced. He had quieted me. I fell asleep.

The next day, the same setup. I sat at a table. A line of probably five hundred people stood before me. The clerk took the book, opened it, placed it in front of me.

This time I was praying as my right hand held the pen. Then I stopped. I looked up, and I saw a beautiful old face. Our eyes locked. My left hand reached out to her face. She lowered her head. I touched her forehead and heard these spontaneous words come out of my mouth while my fingers stroked her brow: "May God bless you where you need the blessing most."

Her eyes filled with tears. As my right hand wrote my name on the open book, I smiled. I shifted the book to the clerk on my right, who closed it and handed it to her.

Now I looked at the next face. I reached out. In the name of God I blessed her, "May the Lord touch you where only *He* can touch you." I saw the eyes suddenly become misty.

Ninety minutes later I was finished. Everyone had received a prayer from their "pastor." The prayer of blessing! Every person got it! A look! A word! A touch! A *blessing!*

"Let's go, Dr. Schuller," my publisher said. "We had five hundred twenty people here today!"

I felt like a true servant of Christ. For an hour and a half I was a human being through whom Jesus Christ had looked, smiled, and blessed human hearts that were so hungry and thirsty for a touch from the living God!

My soul was on the highest mountain peak in its lifetime of adventuring with God in prayer!

## May God Bless You!

I had really learned to pray! It was beautiful!

I was not tired. I was filled with energy! With spiritual power! My life would never be the same. I had learned how to be a blessing by praying the prayer of blessing.

I would repeat this at all the remaining book signings. I would extend the practice in meeting people on sidewalks and in the lobbies of airports around the world.

Even unbelievers let me bless them. I would become a close friend of one of the wealthiest men in the world, a Chinese man from Hong Kong. A Christian? I think not. A believer in God? Not to my knowledge. His name: Sir Y. K. Pau.

Impulsively, I said to him one day when we were alone together at a swimming pool, "I hear you have a serious medical problem?"

He nodded silently. I didn't know that he would die soon and this would be our last time together.

"You know, Sir, I am a Christian. I don't know if you believe in God or know Jesus Christ, but may I give you a blessing?"

He nodded again, approvingly.

I opened the palm of my right hand, reached out to his head, touched his forehead, and heard myself utter these words: "God knows you so much better than you know yourself. He loves you, even if you have never believed in Him. May He reach into a private corner of the secret room in your soul and touch you with the blessing you need and the gift only He can give."

Mr. Pau's famous, brilliant, unemotional eyes suddenly misted over. A warmth radiated between us that I can only describe as "the presence of the Lord." He reached out to grasp affectionately both of my hands, saying, "Thank you! Thank you, Dr. Schuller."

# Prayer in Action

The prayer of blessing! It's prayer in action! Every Christian can be a blessing! You don't need to be a college and seminary graduate! You don't even need to have an education! You simply need to let God do what He wants to do, using your heart, your face, your hands!

After my experience with God on the book-signing tour, I changed the medallion I wore around my neck. I had a new one made, with this prayer carved in gold. I pray it often.

*Lord, lead me to the person*
*You want to speak to*
*Through my life today. Amen.*

# Mother Teresa's Blessing

Mother Teresa and I had never met face-to-face. I had been to her home for the dying in Calcutta, India. We had exchanged letters. Now I was invited to meet her—in person—in Tijuana, Mexico.

I found her surrounded by the poorest of the poor in a pathetic barrio in a suburb of this Mexican border town. She was tiny. Frail. Simple. Saintly.

We connected instantly with a shared spirit I can only describe as "Christ alive in her heart and in mine."

She asked me to repeat the prayer of blessing I had inscribed on a small glass given to every person who had helped build the Crystal Cathedral by buying a window.

"Mother Teresa, your life is an answer to that prayer of blessing," I declared.

"But give it to me anyway," she asked.

I reached out, touched the white cloth that covered her forehead, and, looking into her eyes, prayed the prayer of blessing:

*Lord, make my life*
*A window for Your light*
*To shine through*
*And a mirror to reflect Your love*
*To all I meet. Amen.*

"Write it down for me," she asked.

I did. And then I received one of the greatest honors in my lifetime. Carefully, Mother Teresa, with her small, calloused hands, broken fingernails and all, folded the paper once, and again, and once more. Then she took the thick little wad and reverently, prayerfully slipped it into the folded, private place at the top of her tunic.

"Now you owe me one," I said, smiling. She didn't hesitate a moment. She offered her prayer of blessing on me.

*May you be all,*
*And only, for Jesus,*
*Without Him having*
*To consult you first.*

"Write it down, Mother Teresa," I begged, handing her paper and pen.

She wrote the words and signed her name. Then, with her eyes twinkling with the love of Christ, she handed it to me.

I framed it. It is one of the most prized gifts God has given me.

# Chapter 14

# Hours of Power

Blessed by God so we can be a blessing to others! That's the real meaning of life!

What an honor—to be an ambassador of love and hope while on our soul's adventure!

But I must admit that God's way of doing this is often mysterious and remarkable.

Although my life—like everyone's—has had its share of unexpected twists, one of the most surprising ones is how God would use me and our church to bring His good news to all kinds of people and to all parts of the world—including the atheistic Soviet Union.

When I prayed my first real prayer—"Lord, make me a preacher when I grow up"—I certainly never dreamed my congregation would number in the millions and be scattered across God's good earth!

## The $200,000 Fleece

It was 1969. Billy Graham came to the Anaheim Convention Center for a crusade. I was asked to be vice chairman of the organizing committee. I accepted. There was a large TV truck outside. I was invited to drop in and see how they videotaped the crusade for airing on television.

Billy suggested I televise my church services. "There is no church service on television every Sunday in the Los Angeles market," he said.

"What would it cost?" I asked.

"Probably $400,000 a year," Billy's producer answered.

"But we don't have any spare money!" I replied.

"Try to do what I did when we started my weekly radio program," Billy suggested. "Let God make the decision. When it was suggested I broadcast every week on radio, we put out the fleece and asked God to make the decision. You form a small, secret circle of praying persons."

This was wonderful advice. We took it. We said, "Lord, it'll cost us $400,000 for one year. If people pledge $200,000, that will be your message to go ahead."

I had never, ever, tried praying that way. It was not in my tradition. But I was on an *adventure.* I would try!

I surprised my congregation on Sunday morning when I said, "I've been asked to consider televising our Sunday morning service and airing it every Sunday in Los Angeles. It will cost a lot of money. We don't have a single spare dollar. There is in your program a blank three-by-five card. If you think God wants us to do this, and if you'd be able and willing to help, simply write a dollar amount you would contribute in a twelve-month period. If the total meets half of the annual costs, we'll take that as God telling us He wants us to do it. If the total is a dollar or more less than 50 percent of the annual cost, we'll accept that as God's guidance to pass up this invitation."

We prayed. Passionately.

The cards were dropped in. Many of them. I had no clue what to expect.

"Dr. Schuller." It was our business administrator, Frank Boss, calling me that afternoon. "The total is $189,000. We are $11,000 short of the 50 percent number. It looks like we have our answer."

"But Billy says we have to wait at least for another day or two, because some of the cards may be in the mail," I said. "Perhaps someone wanted to pray with a wife or husband before making the decision."

Although I said this, frankly, I was relieved. It looked like we would not have to consider television!

The next morning Frank Boss called again. "We've just opened the morning mail. We got some more cards like Billy predicted. The total is now $203,000. God has answered our prayers, Bob. He wants us to go on television."

Now—honestly—I was scared.

"Go for it, Bob!" Billy Graham's producer, Fred Dienert, said. "Billy's radio program is evangelism. We call it *Hour of Decision.* Yours will be a church service. Why don't you call it *Hour of Power?*"

Billy Graham had inspired the launching of what would become the first weekly televised church service in California and, soon, the first nationally televised church service in America. Fred Dienert came in to help us plan it.

Yes, I was scared. But enthused about my message—the good news that every person is precious in the sight of God, and every person is created to be an inspiring, blessed, Possibility-Thinking Christian.

## Talent Search in the Kitchen

"We have signed a contract with KTLA, Channel 5, in Los Angeles." It was Fred Dienert, speaking to Frank Boss and me. "Your first program will have to be ready to air the first Sunday of February 1970."

It was early December 1969. The Billy Graham Crusade was three months behind us.

"You will be billed by the station for $4,000 a week," he continued. "They'll send you a bill at the end of every month. The $200,000 pledged will be used to cover the airtime. But the costs of cameras, lighting, monitors, the crew, and the portable recording equipment will cost another $4,000 a week."

"You will have to have the first program recorded and ready to air on the opening Sunday of February or the contract will be canceled," Fred said.

"But I won't need any dollars until we record, right?" I asked.

"Well, first you'll need an executive producer to design the program and choose the music. In short, this person will be the sole designer—call him the architect—to draw the plans in detail," he explained.

"When will we need to hire the executive producer," I asked, "and what's the salary range?"

"When? *Today.* By the middle of January we'll have to tape the first show. We need it recorded three weeks before the first airing on February 5."

"Three weeks?" I asked.

"Yes, Bob, we need three weeks to review the tape, edit the tape, and do all the postproduction work. The cost of the producer? Well, it's a high-bracketed profession. I've got a man in mind, but I'd like you to meet him. It's essential that he is on your wavelength. But we don't really have a day to spare. He'll have to line up talent and writers."

"I'll pray about it, Fred. Part of our problem is we don't have one dollar. All we have are paper promises. And they won't begin to deliver until we do.

"I'll call you back, Fred." I put down the telephone in my bedroom, prayed swiftly, impulsively, and walked to the kitchen and said to Arvella, "I'm willing to go through with TV, but on one condition. That you be the executive producer. You alone. Without having to report to any committee, any board, and not even to me. You'll be accountable to your own mind and heart, where Jesus Christ lives and leads you."

She was standing at the kitchen sink, in shock. "But, Bob, I haven't finished my college work yet. I quit to marry you! And I don't know anything about television!" She was telling the truth.

"But you're smart," I told her. "An A student in high school. I was only a B student! You got straight A's in college. I didn't. The only way I can succeed is to hire people who are smarter than I am! And people whom I love and people whom I can trust 100 percent! And people who understand worship, music, and the requirements our denomination lays down! You qualify.

"And you're the only person I can afford. You'll work for free!"

She laughed. Without further discussion I added a frank comment. "Say 'yes' and so will I. Say 'no' and so will I."

She nodded quietly and humbly accepted the job. She had no idea where this road would lead.

# The Lights Go On

On the Thursday before the Sunday we were to videotape our first service, the church's business manager, Frank Boss, called me and said, "Dr. Schuller, we can't tape Sunday unless the TV lights are installed."

"Okay," I said, "install the lights."

"The electric company has to bring in a new transformer to carry the added . . ."

"Have them do it," I interrupted.

"Bob, they won't do it without being paid," he said.

"Have them send us a bill."

"They won't do it that way. They require a ten-thousand-dollar check up front."

"How much money do we have?" I asked.

"None," he replied. "And I need the check for them by four o'clock this afternoon in order to have the transformers installed and operating by Sunday."

"Wow! We need to pray about this!" I said. "You pray; I'll pray. Maybe we're just not going to be able to go through with it."

This particular Thursday was to be a busy day for me. Now, by four o'clock, I'd have to deliver ten thousand dollars. Where would I get that kind of money? I had no right to take any money from the offerings, which were designated funds. Many appointments would keep me too busy to find some people willing to help buy the lights. My 2:30 appointment was with a name I didn't know. Since both the husband and wife were coming, I assumed they had a marriage problem.

I'll never forget them. The wife was one of the most beautiful women I had ever seen; the husband was a very handsome guy. A striking couple. We had never met.

"Sit down. What's your problem?" I said.

"Oh, Dr. Schuller," he said, "we really don't have a problem. First of all, you should know, we're not members of your church. We're tourists, and we attended church here in November and heard your sermon on tithing. You convinced both of us that it is true. That's what the Bible teaches, and now we really want to do the right thing. So we made a decision to tithe."

I wondered where this conversation was headed.

"We have our own business, and at the end of this past year our accountant reported to us how much money we had made. So we want to tithe on that profit. And you're the one who brought us this message, so we made the check payable to you, Robert Schuller, to use where you need it the most."

Smiling, they handed me a check. It was for ten thousand dollars.

Hours before the deadline we had the cash. And I had the right to spend it how I saw fit. We bought a transformer! The lights were installed, and now we were ready to begin something called *The Hour of Power.* Wow!

ॐ

In 1990, Arvella would produce program one thousand of *The Hour of Power.* The guest list would include all of the living presidents except Jimmy Carter. He had declined the invitation.

Only three weeks before the one thousandth show was to be taped, I wrote former President Carter:

> **Sir, we have never met. I can see why for schedule reasons you'd pass by the invitation to appear on my program along with the four other living presidents. But your absence will create a problem for both you and me—and perhaps for the other four whom I'm committed to air. If you are not on, some**

**will think that you don't like me or that I don't like you or that the other four didn't want a Democrat to be in their circle.**

"I'll do it, Dr. Schuller. If you can come to Plains, Georgia, I'll tape it," President Carter responded. And he did!

The program was aired. Millions viewed it. The first television program in which all five presidents appeared together!

## *The Hour of Power* Expands

When you appear on television, you just never know who might tune in. Over the years, many famous and influential people have thanked us for airing *The Hour of Power*. One of them was Rupert Murdoch.

We met face-to-face for the first time in his office in Beverly Hills. We would meet again at the Crystal Cathedral, where he stood in line with his wife to shake hands with the preacher at the door. We would meet again in his offices in New York and London.

"Bob, I'm putting up the first satellite that will footprint Europe," Rupert told me one day. "I'll turn it on and start European telecasting on the first Sunday of February 1989. And I want one hour—only one hour of religion on that bird when it goes on the air. I want your show to be that hour of religion."

Television airtime was and is very expensive. We were at that time spending over ten million dollars a year for airtime alone. "Thank you, sir," I answered. "But I'm not sure we can afford it."

He smiled. "I'll pay for it. It will be free to you."

So *The Hour of Power* became the first televised church service in history to be aired throughout Europe.

## Friends Connect Again

Only a few years before, I was planning a Sunday when Norman Vincent Peale would be my guest preacher in Garden Grove. It would be his first visit since we had started airing *The Hour of Power* every Sunday over a New York television station.

Having our church service aired in New York City was not easy for Dr. Peale to applaud. This was, after all, his home territory, and we had quickly claimed a sizable weekly audience.

The program aired at 11:00 A.M. on WOR, a powerful station. WOR's management had run into trouble when they had canceled a contract with a Christian-Jewish organization to air a onetime program called "The Passover." Now they were facing a possible lawsuit. To protect themselves, the station offered to sell *The Hour of Power* an hour each week. They probably didn't expect us to accept, but they would have a "no thank you" letter on file from a Christian television ministry. It could serve them well if they were accused of being "anti-Christian."

No TV station in the entire city had ever offered to sell time to a weekly Christian church service. The offer they expected us to reject: four thousand dollars per week for one hour. The contract was for one year. That was almost half of our annual budget, and we had no reserves whatsoever. And we would have to begin on Sunday, July 4, 1971. Starting a new television show on that holiday weekend and at the start of summer was like timing the launching of a ship at the precise hour a hurricane was predicted to hit the coast.

I was never before so *fearful* of a decision. I prayed hard. A Level Four "Let's Connect!" plea.

Should we go on in New York? There was no time to put out a fleece. I asked the three questions I've always asked when facing an exciting, dangerous, positive possibility:

1. Would it be a great thing for God? (The answer must be yes beyond doubt. If not, I'm out of it. No further questions.) I got a solid yes. So I asked the next question.

2. Would it help people who are hurting? (If the answer was no, I'd quit and go no further.) *Yes.* The answer was loud and clear.

But there was one more question I had to ask.

3. Is anybody else doing this? If the answer was yes, then I would hold back. Seldom, if ever, has our church been "the second

or third" in starting new ministries. There is too much to do in our world that no one is doing.

"Let's not compete," I would often tell leaders of the church.

The answer to question three was no, again loud and clear.

The decision was made. We accepted the offer. I signed the contract.

What support could I expect? I asked an old friend. "I think your show is too Californian for New York," he said.

I asked another friend who answered, "Don't quote me, but New York is made up of narrow-minded Catholics, prejudiced Jews, and lukewarm Protestants. No one will support you. Especially coming from California. Maybe Dr. Norman Vincent Peale and the Marble Collegiate Church would televise their service."

A good idea. I met with Dr. and Mrs. Peale.

"Please, Dr Peale, we couldn't turn down this opportunity. But why don't you take it?" He and Ruth were riding with me in a car. I still see their faces, shocked, when they heard of my plan. Both, understandably, showed no enthusiasm.

"No. No, Bob," Dr. Peale answered. "The offer was made to you, not to me. You do it."

Ruth was silent. Was she not the chairman of the board that had paid the young Bob Schuller his first check in 1955 to begin a new church? Now this, in the Peales' home territory?

So I started the first weekly televised church service in the city of New York.

It would be years before the Peales and I would connect again. When we were trying to build the Crystal Cathedral, I would hear Dr. Peale on a national network morning show make uncomplimentary comments about television preachers, and, without naming my name, he made unmistakable negative reference to spending so much money on what I knew was the Crystal Cathedral.

I would be very lonely for his lost friendship for many, many years. I invited him to be a guest preacher to what was now a large TV audience. He declined.

Meanwhile, the New York airing of our show saw a miraculous

response. Within six months viewers were sending voluntary thank-you letters, containing gifts that covered the weekly cost of the airtime.

"Who in the world is supporting *you?*" asked my friend, who had warned me about the people of New York. My answer was a jovial replay of his quote: "Catholics, Jews, and Protestants!"

The viewers were wonderful people! Like a Jewish senator from New York, Jacob Javitz, who found great hope from *The Hour of Power.* He would later be a guest on the program, which was a blessing to him until he died.

As a result of the program, I would be invited to sit in the front row of St. Patrick's Cathedral for Cardinal Spellman's funeral.

And, finally, Dr. Peale would come to respect this effective ministry. I was so grateful when he finally accepted my invitation: "Yes, Bob, I'd be happy to preach for you in the Crystal Cathedral."

We began to prepare for the reunion with Dr. Peale! His return after years of absence created much attention and enthusiasm.

# A Power Connection Begins

"Two weeks and Dr. Peale will be here!" I told my son Robert one day.

"That's great, Dad! You should think about inviting Dr. Armand Hammer to come and hear him."

"Armand Hammer? I remember that name! His father," I explained to Bob, "was one of the six founders of the American Communist Party! I'm not sure he's a prospect to attend our church!"

"Dad," Bob answered, "did you see the picture and read the story of Hammer in this week's *Life* magazine?"

I had. I remained skeptical.

"Remember that huge picture of Dr. Hammer in his bed, looking at three television sets hanging from his ceiling, each tuned to a different network?"

"Yes," I answered. "So?"

"Did you see what magazine was on his bedside table?"

I hadn't noticed.

"Look again, Dad." Bob showed me the *Life* picture.

There it was. Bob was right. On Hammer's bedside table was *Guideposts,* Dr. Peale's popular Christian publication!

I made the move. I wrote the letter and invited Armand Hammer to be our guest and hear—in person—Norman Vincent Peale. I closed my letter, "And if you'd like, you and Dr. Peale could stay for a private luncheon in my office afterwards."

Dr. Armand Hammer telephoned! "Dr. Schuller? I've been watching you for many years. I really enjoy *The Hour of Power.* My wife is a Christian too," he explained. "I'd love to meet you and hear Dr. Peale. I'm happy and honored to accept."

It would be the beginning of a powerful connection between Armand and myself. Our lunch was a wonderful time of friendship building among the three of us. And our relationship with the Peales was warmly reconnected.

Later, both Dr. Peale and Ruth were elected to our international television ministry board. Dr. Peale's positive message would be heard again and again on the largest and longest-running televised church service.

Thank you, Dr. Peale!

Thank You, Lord!

# Broadcasting behind the Communist Curtain

It's 1989.

For nearly six months *The Hour of Power* had aired in Europe. A need was being filled. Murdoch was happy. The prime minister of the Netherlands, Andreas Van Agt, was moved and inspired. He would enthusiastically accept the invitation to serve on our new European television board of directors. He was and is a devout Roman Catholic.

Now it's summer. Armand Hammer is in a European hotel on a Sunday morning. He turns on his television and sees and hears his "pastor," Robert Schuller, in the Crystal Cathedral in Garden Grove. Later, he calls. "How did you get on the air in Europe? It's a message Europe needs!"

"Thank you, Armand." I tell him about Rupert Murdoch launching his Sky Channel only a few months before.

"If Murdoch could get you televised in Europe, I think I can get you televised in the Soviet Union! I'll talk to Gorbachev myself!"

"In the U.S.S.R.?"

I was about to have a new adventure in a country where I'd had such a frightening adventure twenty-one years before.

# "God Loves You, and So Do I"

December 1989. The Soviet Union. Arvella and I had been flown into the country with Armand Hammer, a man who was loved and respected by Soviets. We had one purpose—to investigate the possibility of delivering *The Hour of Power* to the entire populace of the U.S.S.R., including all of the Eastern Bloc countries.

The possibility was overwhelming. I found it hard to believe that it could ever happen. I had returned to the country where I was once branded an "Enemy of the State." And now I was exploring the possibility of preaching to those same people on their state-controlled television network.

Armand Hammer felt that I was the person who could open Soviet eyes to the idea of a positive faith.

But first we had to meet with the power people. I had to be interviewed privately, to see if I met their approval.

Twenty years earlier, I had smuggled my faith into the country. This time I arrived with Dr. Armand Hammer in his private jet with Gorbachev's personal approval. Our VIP transport bypassed usual immigration and custom procedures.

A huge limousine waited at curbside. We drove to the Occidental Petroleum office, where Dr. Hammer had one of only five telephones in the whole country that could be used to make a direct, instantaneous international call. After he called home to check on his wife, we headed for Gostelradio—the formal power center where all control of Russian Communist programming was exercised.

We were welcomed royally and escorted to the central command headquarters headed by Valentin Lazutkin. The office featured a large conference table. Lazutkin sat directly across the table from Dr. Hammer. I sat on Hammer's right side, and Arvella sat next to me. On Hammer's left side sat his chief aide, Rick Jacobs. A tray of sweets and soft drinks separated us from the Russian power people.

Lazutkin smiled, drew his calling card from his pocket, and handed one to each of us. Dr. Hammer then offered his card to Lazutkin, who smiled proudly as he accepted the card from the most respected, honored, and trusted American in all of Russia.

Dr. Hammer opened the meeting by introducing me. "I have been coming to this country since Lenin came to power. I have informed Gorbachev of my coming here today to ask for Dr. Schuller to be invited to share his message of hope and faith with this entire nation, all fifteen of the republics of the U.S.S.R., and all of the eight Eastern Bloc nations. I think the time has come for your broadcasting media to be opened to religion."

The chain-smoking Lazutkin showed no emotion. He answered crisply, "You know, of course, that the television empire was created to teach all people what we believe. We are an atheistic country—the first nation to be so enlightened. This Channel One is on Sputnik, the only satellite that instantly footprints the entire globe. How can we suddenly allow this to be used to proclaim religion?"

After a pause, Lazutkin continued: "But after seventy years of atheism, we have come to see that certain positive traits in human personality only seem to come through religious roots. So we are open to review our atheistic policy and seriously look at religion. However, what religion is safe? And responsible? And how can we avoid religious conflicts?

"We have the Orthodox Church, Roman Catholics, Pentecostals, Jews, plus fifty million Muslims. They all disagree and are in conflict!" Then turning to me he asked, "What denomination do you belong to?"

When I replied that I belonged to the Reformed Church in America, he responded, "Oh!" Then he studied me more closely and continued, "The Reformed Church is well known and respected in Europe and Eastern Europe.

"But we have never, in our seventy years of communism, allowed any foreigner to use our broadcasting to talk about God. That is impossible."

Lazutkin looked at Hammer. He knew that in Russia when Dr. Hammer asked for *anything,* you could not give him a flat no. How could he resolve the historic contradiction he faced?

"Dr. Hammer, I could have our Sunday evening Russian 'Barbara Walters' interview Dr. Schuller as a guest from Dr. Hammer's office. She could ask him what he does. She could say, 'Dr. Schuller, do you preach sermons about God on American and European TV? Give us a sample!' Then Dr. Schuller could preach for—maybe 15 minutes."

Lazutkin looked at me. I nodded approval. He reached out. We shook hands.

"Dr. Schuller, you can know you made history as the first foreigner to preach on Russian TV."

I was "in" with official approval!

Lazutkin concluded, "Dr. Hammer says you have good things to say to the people of the Soviet Union. Let's walk down to a studio and record it now."

He stood up. We rose. As his strong hand grasped mine, he said, "I must tell you something, Dr. Schuller. I will let you talk about God on television, but I don't believe in Him. I have never experienced God."

I looked this man in the eye and said, "Oh! But you have! You have experienced God many times. You just didn't recognize Him. That time when you felt love for your wife or your daughter. That time when you held back a tear because you were touched by an emotion that seemed to come from nowhere—that was God. You just didn't call it by the right name."

Lazutkin's eyes glistened for a moment. In one miraculous moment I saw the spark of the Spirit of God in his eyes! He was forever changed—then and there! Years have passed, but now he concludes his letters to me with, "God loves you, and so do I."

Arvella and I were both excited about the opportunity to speak to the Soviet people, but I was nervous. What would I say? Would they want to screen my message ahead of time? I had heard how strictly every message was controlled. It was common practice for all scripts to be submitted ahead of time for censorship purposes. How would my message be handled?

Just then we were told to report immediately to the television station located on the floor above Lazutkin's office. We were quickly ushered to the studio, where I was met by their "Barbara Walters," a lovely, popular Soviet reporter named Natalia. We chatted briefly. Then she said, "We have decided that we will do a short interview with you, then I will turn the platform over to you. You will have fifteen minutes to address the Soviet people. Are you ready?"

Now? Right now? I looked around. There was the director. Cameramen were adjusting their cameras. The lights were being snapped on. An audio technician clamped a microphone on my tie. I gulped, "Sure! I'm ready!" But secretly I prayed with a passion. "What am I going to say? Lord, help!"

Natalia turned to the camera and began her introduction. It was in Russian, but the interpreter translated instantly into the earphone I was wearing. I heard her say, "Good evening. We start today's program in a rather unusual manner. It will be a little longer. And we have a rather unusual guest.

"On his most recent trip to the Soviet Union, Dr. Armand Hammer, the famous American businessman, invited his friend Pastor Robert Schuller to come with him. Pastor Schuller is a preacher with the Reformed Church in California. He is very well known to Americans because he delivers a sermon on television every week.

"Dr. Schuller, where did the idea of televising a sermon in America come from?"

Fortunately, my reply was taped, otherwise I never would have remembered how I answered Natalia. I said, "Well, I started a brand-new church with my wife, just the two of us, and it grew faster and faster. We built a church that could hold 1,500 people, but after ten years we had outgrown it. There just wasn't room for all the people. So we started televising the services. That way, people who could not get out to go to church could see it in their homes or in the hospitals."

Next question: "What is your sermon based on? What is the most important element for you?"

I said, "One concept. Call it encouragement. Hope. Self-confidence and enthusiasm for life. Everything we do in our ministry, in our messages, in our music, in our architecture, is to restore balance to people's lives. I can live without pleasure, but I can't live in shame. People cannot humiliate me; they cannot strip me of my dignity, unless I allow them to. I have a life, and I'm proud of who I am. And that's true for every living human being. And that is the essence of what religion is all about—finding and giving people back their dignity."

Natalia then asked, "When you are preaching your sermon, do you intend it only for believers, or do you address it to the entire American people, and now the whole world, to believers and non-believers?"

"That's a wonderful question," I replied. "It's why I'm different from many other religious spokespersons. I'm primarily interested in talking to people who don't have religion. People who have religion already have a place to worship."

"I see," said Natalia. "And tell me, do you think—and if so, why?—that both nonbelievers and believers all over the world need this sermon?"

"I think that any human being needs affirmation and encouragement. Every single person, every day, meets some disappointment. And we can't allow that disappointment to grow into discouragement. So, I think everybody needs hope. Everybody needs enthusiasm. And everybody, every day, needs to have their spirit lifted."

Next question: "Dr. Schuller, are you convinced that our people will understand what you have to say to them?"

"Oh, yes. Because I know people, and people are the same all over the world. They have dreams, they have hurts, they have memories—some good memories and some bad memories. They like babies; they like love. All human beings are the same. That's my specialty. And the Bible, God, and Jesus Christ tell me how I can treat people beautifully, and they will understand."

Then Natalia did a remarkable thing. She turned to me and said,

"Then I will leave you and the Soviet people alone together. Please, go ahead. Talk to them from your heart."

I gulped. I had no time to think; the red light of the camera was on. Every moment was being recorded. I had been given the opportunity to talk to the Soviet people, uncensored. But I had no time to prepare my thoughts. I had to speak now—the only problem was—what was I going to say?

I sensed an enormous responsibility to represent "religion." My role would be that of a "ground breaker." If I left a good impression, it could open the door to more religious programming. If I left a negative impression, then the door might remain closed—perhaps forever!

I prayed and believed that the God who had given me the "gift of tongues" would not fail me now. "Remember, Dr. Schuller," Lazutkin had said, "you will be listened to by all of the government leaders and more than two hundred million people. Everyone will want to hear this first foreigner preaching a sermon! We will air this on this coming December 25, 1989, from 9:00 to 9:30 P.M. on Channel One, the world's most powerful television channel!"

My opening words came out: "I cannot begin to thank you for this wonderful honor. I would like to share some thoughts with you, my brothers and sisters in the Soviet Union. It's Christmas time, and Christmas is when we remember the words of Jesus, 'Peace I give to you.'

"I'm so excited, because Christmas 1989 marks the first time in this century that the people of the United States of America and Russia are beginning to trust each other.

"I have a confession to make: There has been a great deal of distrust between our countries. At least, we have been guilty of it. There was a great distrust—until something happened very recently. Our president, George Bush, met with your president, Mikhail Gorbachev. They sat together, shoulder to shoulder, in a live, globally televised news conference. When the American people saw that, there was a birth of trust on a level I have never experienced or known.

"And so, I can say to you that the American people want to trust the Russian people, and that's so beautiful, because trust sets the stage for real love. Real love, comradeship, harmony, and peace are never possible between two persons or between two countries unless first there's trust.

"So we're ready to step into a new era. The 1990s, I predict, will be a decade of peace. The next millennium will soon come, and we will all—in the Soviet Union and in America—look forward to each day, each tomorrow, without fear.

"So I have a special gift for you, a very beautiful gift. It is a promise, a prophecy from the Bible. In the Old Testament, in Jeremiah 29:11, God speaks: 'For I know the plans I have for you. . . . They are plans for good and not for evil, to give you a future and a hope' (TLB).

"Never have we been able to look forward to tomorrow with such hopefulness, such optimism. Think of it—the wars that people were afraid might come will never come. The nuclear bombs are all going to be dismantled.

"We stand on the edge of a wonderful time in history. Television programs are broadcast from the Soviet Union to America and from America to the Soviet Union. With satellites in the sky, we are able to talk to each other, understand each other, care about each other, give hope to each other, love each other—that's our tomorrow.

"Now, you say to me, 'Prove to me that there is a God.'

"And I say, 'When so much good is happening, you prove to me that there is no God.'

"You say, 'What is God?'

"And I say, 'He is not flesh and bones, but rather He is Spirit.'

"And how can you experience Him? You experience Him when an idea comes to your mind. Where does the idea come from? It's a creative idea; it's a wonderful idea. Maybe the idea can become a song. Maybe the idea can become an invention. Maybe the idea can become a breakthrough in negotiations so that people who are hostile become friendly."

I witnessed—I did not preach! I shared my story. I talked about my children. I shared the story of my daughter Carol and her amputation. "She only lost a leg. She did not lose her faith in God!

"Today, twelve years later, that beautiful girl is married and has two little children. She is very happy. Do you know what she would say if she were here today? She would say what I said earlier, from the Bible: 'I have a plan for your life, a plan for good, not evil, a plan to give you a future with hope.'

"You can choose either to be a skeptic or a believer. Birds were meant to fly. Flowers were meant to bloom. Humans were designed to believe in beauty, in love, in truth, in God. Does God exist? Is He good? Open your mind to the idea. After all, if one entire country can open its mind to the possibility that faith is the only answer, faith is the only hope, then maybe you can open your mind to this exciting possibility. Take a look around you. More people believe in a good God everyday. Maybe you should too.

"Just because you don't believe in God doesn't mean He's not working with you. You may call it a mood shift. You don't recognize it was God. You may have thought that you got a bright idea. You didn't recognize it was God. You thought, *What a lucky break.* You didn't realize it was God.

"How do you recognize God? Be alert to Him. Give Him a chance to come into your life. Take one tiny step right here and right now. Open your heart. Just a tiny, tiny crack. Be brave enough to think, *Maybe there is a God. Maybe He does love me. Maybe He will get me through my problems too. Maybe, just maybe, I can dream again!*

"My friends, thank you. Have a blessed and prosperous new year. In 1990, you and I will become friends. America and Russia will help each other. We will become comrades in peace, hope, and freedom.

"I don't understand or speak Russian, but I have a famous American saying, and I want to see if I can say it in Russian:

"Bog Lubit Vas I Ya Tozhe!

"In English, it's 'God loves you, and so do I.'

"Bog Lubit Vas I Ya Tozhe!"

That message was aired as promised all across the Soviet Union at 9:00 P.M., December 25, 1989. I heard from some of the leaders in the Soviet Union, including Gorbachev, that the message was enthusiastically received.

Lazutkin sent a wire telling me that over two hundred million people had viewed the program.

Five months later, I was invited by Lazutkin to tape another sermon for the Soviets.

I did. The program aired the night before Gorbachev left for a summit meeting in Washington. My message followed a message from Gorbachev and a taped greeting from President Bush. My text was: "And now abide faith, hope, love, these three; but the greatest of these is love" (1 Cor. 13:13).

I was invited to have lunch with Gorbachev in Washington.

In front of the CNN cameras broadcasting live from the Russian embassy, Gorbachev pointed me out as the "American preacher whose message brought a greater calm to my nation than even my message did."

Next came an invitation to broadcast the entire *Hour of Power* translated into Russian every Sunday as the first and only Christian church service on Channel One. The first nationally televised church service to be heard every week across the U.S.S.R.!

Prayer! "Lord, make me a blessing," I prayed. What an answer He delivered!

# In Lenin's Apartment

Friday, April 30, 1993. I was back in Moscow, meeting with Mikhail Gorbachev in his office.

This was a historic week in Russia. Only five days ago, on Sunday, April 25, the nation had had its first free election for a president!

For more than a thousand years, Russia had been a Christian nation, but emperors and czars had ruled. It was never a democracy.

Then in 1917, Lenin and communism took over. Then came Gorbachev and Peristroika.

"Dr. Schuller—I put you on Russian TV," Gorbachev said. "Now you have been on for one hour every week the entire past year. And

I am off TV completely!" While we visited, a call came from Boris Yeltsin's office in the Kremlin. It was his associate chief of staff asking me to come to his office.

Yeltsin had won. Now I was invited to his headquarters in the Kremlin.

I was welcomed and then escorted through doors, down halls, deep into the inner sanctum where communist world power was centered for most of this tumultuous atomic century.

"Step in, Dr. Schuller," Yeltsin's aide said warmly. "My wife never misses your television program. Every Sunday for a year, you have been on Channel One. There's hardly a citizen in Russia or in the other republics who hasn't heard your message."

His office was huge. Several chairs, a large desk with about twenty telephones, and a thirty-six-inch television hung high on the wall.

With moist eyes the chief of staff added, "Dr. Schuller, you don't realize that your message is as radical in this nation's culture and history as the message from Karl Marx on collectivism was when it hit us seventy-five years ago!" Reaching out now to grab my shoulders, he said, "Dr. Schuller, you are to be thanked for giving our people faith, hope, and love."

I didn't know how to handle that one! I felt awkwardly embarrassed—but proud. "By the way," I said "I've never been here in the heart of the Kremlin before. Isn't this where Lenin had his office?"

He nodded yes. I went on, "You know my friend Armand Hammer told me he gave a gift to Lenin, a small bronze statue. He told me it's still on Lenin's desk in the Kremlin. Is that true?"

He laughed, picked up a phone, and gave a command I couldn't understand. He turned. "Follow me, Dr. Schuller."

We walked out the door, up one flight of stairs, and at the end of the hall we came to a locked door. He pressed numbers on a small combination lock. The door was opened by a small, gray-haired, professorial gentleman.

"Welcome, Dr. Schuller, to the private residence of Vladimir Lenin," the man said with a smile. "Dr. Schuller, this is a historic day for us. It was seventy-five years ago today—April 30, 1918—that Lenin moved in and walked through this door. Now seventy-five years later, you, a minister of Christianity, enter to a warm welcome! Please sign our guest register."

I signed my name, noted the date, and left a penned prayer of blessing.

"Now let me show you through Lenin's private apartment. You'll see his kitchen, bedroom, office, and the cabinet room. Everything is left exactly as it was the day he died. The dishes on the kitchen table are still here. Follow me," he said.

We moved down the hall. The first door led to a bedroom with a single bed, dresser, and desk. "Mrs. Lenin's bedroom," he said.

As we continued the tour, Yeltsin's chief of staff whispered, "Dr. Schuller, this man is the leading authority in the world on Lenin! Any questions, ask him."

The adjoining room was another small bedroom. There was only a single bed. "This is Lenin's bed," he said. "And that is his desk."

I looked. No bronze statue. The next room was a small library with a desk and chair. "This was Lenin's private library of his favorite books. Dr. Schuller, look at the full shelves. Now look at that red book on the eye level of Lenin within reach of his arm when he sat in his chair." And the professor reached, picked it out, and handed it to me. In Russian, *The Life of Christ.*

"Dr. Schuller, Lenin was fifteen years old and thinking of becoming a priest in the Orthodox Church when a clergy-teacher said in class, 'The cross is a symbol of human suffering. Suffering is good. Even children must grow up learning that.'

"At that point Lenin reached in his shirt, grabbed the gold cross around his neck, ripped it off, threw it on the floor, and angrily announced, 'Then I will have none of it.' He became an atheist then and there."

The professor carefully returned the book to the shelf, turned to me, and said, "Dr. Schuller, if you or another positive Christian clergy would have been his teacher, he'd have grown up a follower of Jesus."

I looked at the desk. No bronze statue on his private desk and none in his library. The next room was a living room, with a sofa, a small grand piano, a phonograph with a recording of Beethoven. Another desk. No bronze statue.

"Lenin had his 'oval office' too. It's down the hall next to his cabinet room. Follow me."

The door at the end of the hall was open. It was, in fact, a small oval office. The walls were covered with maps showing the battle lines in the country the day he died.

"There were still sections of our country not under his control," my host explained. He pointed to another desk. "This was his seat of power. This is where he ruled from," he said. And there on the desk was the bronze statue! Twelve inches high.

"This was a gift from his American friend, Armand Hammer! It's never been off the desk, where he placed it when Dr. Hammer gave it to him—here in this, his office!" It was true. Dr. Hammer really *did* know Lenin.

A door was open to a large, narrow room. A table surrounded by what looked to be twenty chairs filled most of the room's space. One head chair was larger than the others.

"This is the cabinet room. Lenin presided from this head chair. Everyone you've ever heard about in the leadership of this country in over seventy years of communism sat in one of these chairs. Stalin sat there. Kruschev sat there. They all sat there. But that's all history! Lenin is dead. And they're all gone or out of power today."

I could hardly sleep that night. I prayed, "Thank You, God. You did it! You answered my prayer. You really did make me a preacher when I grew up."

Prayer! The changes in the Soviet Union were an answer to prayer. Whose prayers? Yours? Mine? Prayers prayed by Christians around the world for decades? Yes! Yes! Yes!

Amen! And Hallelujah!

# A Special Blessing from God

As I finish this book I have just had a profoundly moving experience that stands apart from any and all experiences in my life.

I have had private meetings with heads of state, with the presidents of the United States, and, a few times, with Pope John Paul II.

But my recent experience stands apart as, I believe, God's special gift to this minister.

It was something this Possibility Thinker never would have believed could happen to me!

I spent an afternoon, a night, and a morning in what may be the most revered bed and bedroom in America.

The president of the United States invited me to spend the night in Lincoln's bedroom at the White House, Monday, February 13, 1995, the day officially set aside by the country to celebrate Lincoln's birthday.

Only a week before, I had planned to be in the capital. And when President Clinton heard that I would be there, I received an invitation to "be the president's overnight guest in the White House." This followed a private telephone conversation on Christmas Eve 1994, when the president called me, and, after prayer, said, "Next time you're in Washington, come and see me."

Now I was invited to spend a night in the White House. But a horrible storm swept through the capital. Plane flights were canceled. So on Sunday, February 5, I had to call the White House to cancel.

"We'll try to put something together later," I was told.

The next week I was scheduled to attend a board meeting in Jamaica. I called my office from Jamaica. "I'll catch a flight to Washington Sunday afternoon. I'll be able to be in the Capitol Monday and Tuesday. If at all possible, I'd like private meetings with my friends in both political parties."

I was thrilled with the report that came back. "Dr. Schuller, you have private appointments on Monday and Tuesday with Senators Bob Dole, Diane Feinstein, Mark Hatfield, Orin Hatch, and Byron Dorgan. The minority speaker in the Senate, Thomas Daschle, and Newt Gingrich, Speaker of the House, will meet you too. And the president is asking you again to spend Monday night in the White House. Dr. Schuller, the president wants to invite you to sleep in the same room where Lincoln slept!"

Carolyn Huber, the special assistant to the president, met me at the White House south entrance. We boarded the elevator and stopped on floor two. That entire floor is the private home for the first family. There was the president's private bedroom, with his door opening to a long wide hallway furnished like a living room. Next to the president's bedroom door is the door to the president's private office, which he can enter from a side door that connects to his private sleeping quarters.

The next doors, two of them, enter Lincoln's bedroom. Carolyn Huber opened the last door. "This leads to a short hall with a private bath, and a private Lincoln living room with desk, sofa, and fireplace. Use all the stationery you want, Dr. Schuller. Write your family and friends a letter from the White House."

(Wonderful advice. I handwrote forty-four letters to my children, grandchildren, and special friends.)

Then Carolyn led me to a door on one side of the living room. She opened it, smiled, and gestured to the open doorway. "This, Dr. Schuller, is Lincoln's bedroom! This is yours this afternoon, tonight, and tomorrow morning."

My face twitched, my lips quivered, my voice broke with profound emotions as I softly said, "Thank you."

In the room was the famous, high-backed, extralong Lincoln bed, more than thirty square feet in size. Every president since Lincoln had slept in that bed, and I would sleep in that same bed that night! It stands against the east wall, facing the fireplace, which has a bronzed plate on the mantel that reads: "In this room Abraham Lincoln signed the Emancipation Proclamation, setting four million slaves free." Theodore Roosevelt, who loved sleeping in this extralong and wide bed, had the plate added during his administration.

The antique desk stands on the south wall between windows overlooking the grand lawn. Above the desk, framed under glass, is the Gettysburg address, written in Abraham Lincoln's own hand!

My imagination stirred. One hundred thirty years ago Lincoln was *here!* This was his special room! Here he pondered, laughed, cried, and prayed.

To be in such a place on such a special day was a special blessing from God; there was no doubt about it. Carolyn Huber had said to me, just before she left me alone, "Oh, Dr. Schuller. We were so happy you had to cancel coming here last Monday, because this bedroom was being renovated, and you'd have been assigned to an official guest bedroom on the upper floor of the White House."

God was in the storm!

God had me in mind when He led me to cancel my visit to the White House a week earlier.

After this experience, I'll never be the same person. God wanted me to *feel* the history through which I have been blessed, a history without which I could not have served Him as I have.

Thank You, Lord!

# POSITIVE PRAYER... IT'S IMMORTAL!

*I'm destined to be decisive.*

"AND THE TIME OF THE SINGING OF BIRDS HAS COME."
— SONG 2:12, TLB —

# Positive Prayer... It's Immortal!

nd where is my soul today in its adventure with God? What passage in the Holy Bible consumes my consciousness now with greater force than any other passage in the Scriptures? It is the fifteenth chapter of St. John's Gospel. These words of Jesus are addressed to the person who has lived a life of prayer.

"I AM THE TRUE VINE, AND MY FATHER IS THE VINEDRESSER. . . . I AM THE VINE, YOU ARE THE BRANCHES. HE WHO ABIDES IN ME, AND I IN HIM, BEARS MUCH FRUIT; FOR WITHOUT ME YOU CAN DO NOTHING. . . . IF YOU ABIDE IN ME, AND MY WORDS ABIDE IN YOU, YOU WILL ASK WHAT YOU DESIRE, AND IT SHALL BE DONE FOR YOU. BY THIS MY FATHER IS GLORIFIED, THAT YOU BEAR MUCH FRUIT. . . . NO LONGER DO I CALL YOU SERVANTS . . . BUT I HAVE CALLED YOU FRIENDS. . . . YOU DID NOT CHOOSE ME, BUT I CHOSE YOU AND APPOINTED YOU THAT YOU SHOULD GO AND BEAR FRUIT, AND THAT YOUR FRUIT SHOULD REMAIN, THAT WHATEVER YOU ASK THE FATHER IN MY NAME HE MAY GIVE YOU." (JOHN 15:1, 5, 7–8, 15–16)

So I come to the twilight years of my life knowing that I have had, I *do* have, I *will* have beyond my lifetime real value and worth in divine destiny: "You did not choose Me, but I chose you."

So I have a healthy, humble, hopeful, and helpful self-esteem today!

In my childhood I was chosen last when sides were drawn to play ball during school recess. This early rejection instilled a low level of self-appraisal, and again and again in life I saw myself as being on the outside.

I often have been rejected, passed by, and even openly criticized in print and from the platform by power people in religious circles, as well as by those who are influential in broader society. From time to time I hoped for but did not receive invitations to serve on honorary boards or to speak from significant platforms.

But now I can see it clearly. *I am a chosen person!* Picked by God to be His ambassador in the world, representing His Son, my Savior, Jesus Christ!

"You did not choose Me, but I chose you." At this stage of my life hardly a day passes when these words don't come strongly to my mind. I'm well aware that my life was and is a divine destiny. But I was destined to be decisive. I decided to embrace the faith and live a life of sincere prayer.

When your self-esteem is rooted in a divine destiny and in a heavenly relationship with Christ, your pride will be safe and satisfying while your humility will be sure and sweet. Hallelujah and amen!

# The Two Mysterious Levels of Prayer

Here—now—as I finish this book—I have a new and fresh perspective on my full life of positive prayer.

I now see that there are two mystery levels of prayer—two levels we are only now discovering in these closing pages. We can detect and define these levels, but we cannot describe them in detail, for they are the forms and faces of prayer that precede our birth and continue beyond our lifetime. They remain mysteries of past, present, and future history. Call them the Ancestral and Descendant Levels.

## The Ancestral Level

My life—and your life—is an answer to more prayers than we will ever know. Many were prayed before we were born. Are you and

I living a life that in the final analysis is a vast collection of prayers offered and answered through the years? There are countless "live files" of prayers that were prayed for decades—even centuries—before we were born that are still being answered to our blessed benefit! Like fruit trees that bear fruit generation after generation, long after the person who planted them has passed on.

I recall a visit I made to Norman and Ruth Peale's home in Pawling, New York, shortly before Norman's death. The lovely house and the gardens are quite old. The spacious estate was created by dreamers, landscape and structural architects, and developers—people who are now long gone.

"You've got to see the old apple tree, Bob," Norman said. He was more than ninety years old as he slowly walked me through the sprawling country estate. We headed for one solitary old tree. It was not large. It was obviously very, very old. Scars marked the place on the tree where longer and larger branches apparently had been removed decades ago. The trunk was no longer full and fat and round. Instead, it was shaped more like a quarter moon, with most of the once round and filled-out trunk now hollowed out from the ground up. A child could stand up in the hollowed-out trunk. But one side of the tree, from the roots up, was still alive and strong and covered with healthy bark that was feeding and keeping alive two smaller, younger, fruit-bearing branches!

"How old is it?" I asked.

"I have no idea," Dr. Peale answered. "It was here when we moved here. It may be two hundred years old!"

## The Life Span of a Prayer

What is the life span of a tree? A family? A nation? A book? An idea? A prayer?

"Any fool," I wrote in one of my books, "can count the seeds in an apple, but only God can count the apples in one seed."

When my mother and father passed away, their possessions and property and invested prayers did not die with them! "Living assets" remained to be distributed and *passed on,* not passed away! Like an old remnant of an ancient fruit tree, many rich inheritances from our ancestors are still alive, sprouting new branches and bearing fresh fruit! The way the old apple tree still lives in the Peales' garden.

Are many of my great-great-grandparents' prayers still alive, blessing generation after generation?

God declared this paradigm of perpetuity when He said to Abraham (Genesis 17) that his seed would be blessed—and the seed after him—in an everlasting covenant.

None of us knows his whole history. Hundreds of years ago, one of our ancestors may have been saved from a shipwreck, a battle, or an epidemic.

If my grandfather, John Schuller, had been killed when he fell under a runaway team of horses pulling a wagon of coal, I would have "died" before I was born, because my father would not have been conceived.

I know that my father's prayer for a son preceded my conception. I know that maternal and paternal grandparents prayed before my father and my mother were born.

All humans alive today, if they could trace their ancestry back, generation after generation, would encounter a miracle moment when their lineage was miraculously spared from extinction of some sort. Not a single one of us would have even been born if it were not for the prayers that preserved and perpetuated our bloodline and brought us into existence. The Ancestral Level of prayer.

# The Descendant Level

Then there is the level of our prayer life that I call the Descendant Level. We will never know how our prayers will shape the lives of our children and our children's children long after we're gone. This level, too, will remain a mystery of history waiting to unfold in God's tomorrows.

I have seventeen grandchildren. I prayed for each of them before they were born. "Let them be born," I prayed, "to live a long and blessed life."

I have prayed that prayer for all of them throughout their entire lives! As late as only a few hours ago!

Their parents pray the same prayers. So does their grandmother. And all of these thousands of accumulated and compounding prayers add up to numbers that boggle the mind. (Count 365 prayers a year and in only ten years they add up to 3,650 prayers from Grandpa alone!) And these prayers are not drops of dew on morning grass. They are not snowflakes before a warm and rising sun. All are fertile seeds planted in God's eternal garden. In His timing the fruit of blessing will ripen.

He keeps the family prayer files open long after we are gone. Yes, we will someday stop praying, but God will keep on answering!

We plant seeds in God's garden, and their fruit in generations yet unborn will become a part of the divine destiny of creativity.

Our decisions to pray are a primal factor in divine destinies yet to be fulfilled.

# God Never Quits Answering Prayer

"Lord, make me a preacher when I grow up."

As I finish telling of my soul's adventure with God, I am struck with a new thought: "When did I stop praying that prayer?" Did I stop praying it when, twenty years later, I graduated from seminary? I passed all the tests. I earned all my degrees. I was examined, licensed, and ordained by my denomination! Of course, the prayer was answered.

Now I have a revelation.

I stopped praying that prayer, but God never stopped answering it!

When we send our prayers to God, we are casting seeds into His garden. Some are petunias. They sprout, grow, bloom, and that's it. But others are perennial; they blossom, die out in winter, but come back in spring to bloom year after year. Still others are trees—like the walnut tree—with life spans of seventy years or more in which to bear their fruit. And perhaps one or two are seeds of trees that have a virtually unending life span—like the olive tree or the giant California redwood. We may stop praying, but God will keep on answering the prayer, season after season, century after century.

Now I see it! My childhood prayer! I planted it! God blessed it, and He is still working on it. My mistake? I quit praying it too soon! But He didn't quit on me.

So on a recent Sunday, at the age of 68, I started all over again. As I prepared to climb the fifteen steps from my office to the pulpit to preach at the Crystal Cathedral, I heard myself utter the words, "Make me a preacher, Lord, when I *go* up. Amen."

So what's the life span of our prayers? Only God knows. Many prayers, I am sure, will be immortal.

And my future? I am sure God is planning surprises for me in my tomorrows that will be answers to prayers prayed days or decades ago!

This promise of Christ I truly believe: "Whoever lives and believes in Me shall never die" (John 11:26).

# *About the Author*

Robert H. Schuller began his ministry with two members and five hundred dollars in a drive-in theater in California in 1955. Today his face is seen by more people every week than any other religious leader in the world. He is the founder and spokesman on America's television church, *The Hour of Power,* which is the longest running and the most widely viewed televised church service in the United States. It was the first televised church service to cover all of America, and the first televised church service seen in Europe, Korea, Australia, and Russia.

Every year hundreds of millions of people are introduced to his message from the world-renowned Crystal Cathedral, home of what is today the largest congregation in the oldest Protestant denomination with a continuous ministry in the United States of America—the Reformed Church in America.

Dr. Schuller is the author of thirty books, five of which were on the *New York Times* and *Publisher's Weekly* best-seller lists. *Prayer: My Soul's Adventure with God,* his thirtieth book, is his first autobiography. His lifetime involvement in architecture, psychology, theology, and motivation seminars make him a true "Renaissance man." He lives with his wife, Arvella, in Garden Grove, California.